DO THIS IN REMEMBRANCE OF ME

Do This in Remembrance of Me

A Ritual Approach
to Reformed Eucharistic Theology

Martha L. Moore-Keish

William B. Eerdmans Publishing Company

Grand Rapids, Michigan / Cambridge, U.K.

Published 2008 by

Wm. B. Eerdmans Publishing Co.

2140 Oak Industrial Drive N.E., Grand Rapids, Michigan 49505 /

P.O. Box 163, Cambridge CB3 9PU U.K.

Printed in the United States of America

12 11 10 09 08   7 6 5 4 3 2 1

Library of Congress Cataloging-in-Publication Data

Moore-Keish, Martha L.

Do this in remembrance of me:

a ritual approach to Reformed Eucharistic theology /

Martha L. Moore-Keish.

p.   cm.

Includes bibliographical references.

ISBN 978-0-8028-6244-0 (pbk.: alk. paper)

1. Lord's Supper — Reformed Church.

2. Reformed Church — Doctrines — History.   I. Title.

BX9423.C5M66   2008

234′.63 — dc22

2007043714

www.eerdmans.com

Contents

Preface

This book began as a doctoral dissertation. As such, it represents an initial foray into several conversations, and an attempt to bring those conversations to bear on one another. It grew out of lively seminar discussions, long hours at the library and the coffee shop, breathtaking discoveries of whole new fields of study, and arduous journeys through those fields, sometimes accompanied, sometimes alone.

Though this book grew out of a particular academic exercise, in a more profound way it grew out of a deep hunger for encounter with the triune God. It represents my growing conviction that this hunger is both intensified and satisfied when I come to the Lord's Supper with my whole self, expecting to meet Christ. My hunger, then, has two dimensions: an awareness of absence (in this case, an absence in my own theological tradition that too often has denied or feared the power of ritual), and a conviction that in the ritual celebration of the Lord's table I encounter the presence of the living God who satisfies my desire. In a way, this entire project is an invitation to fuller participation in the eucharistic feast.

As an interdisciplinary endeavor, this project has both benefits and limitations. One benefit is that it brings scholars from several different fields into conversation with each other, helping those who work in the area of theology to overhear a bit of the discussion carried on by ritual theorists, and inviting those who work in ritual to glimpse some of what liturgical theologians argue about most passionately.

Yet such a project also has its limits. It cannot address with care all of the relevant important scholarly conversations in current literature, like the historical development of Calvin's thought, new proposals for understanding sacramental presence, and detailed debates among ritual and performance theorists. Furthermore, this project raises questions that it cannot always answer. For instance, I suggest but do not work out fully in this essay the complex relationship between the work of the Spirit and the principle of emergence as developed by performance theorists. I hope those who are interested will read further in the scholarly literature regarding particular questions, and will propose answers themselves to questions I raise.

Despite its limitations, I do hope this book will spark the imagination and contribute to a conversation between two groups who sometimes regard each other with mutual suspicion: those who regard "ritual" as either irrelevant to theology or a dangerous distraction from it, and those who think ritual is the most fascinating of human endeavors.

Many teachers, friends, and colleagues have helped bring this book to birth. Don Saliers and Rebecca Chopp served as co-advisers to the dissertation, and I am grateful for their persistent questions, illuminating guidance, and gracious affirmation. Thanks are also due to other important teachers in the Graduate Division of Religion at Emory, especially Wendy Farley, Walter Lowe, and Joyce Flueckiger, who in many and varied ways enabled me better to read, to see, and to question. Jim Farwell, Siobhan Garrigan, and Paul Galbreath have been significant friends and conversation partners along the way, as I have wrestled with all of these questions. I am grateful for folks who have read and commented on earlier drafts of this work, especially Stan Hall, Douglas Ottati, John Witvliet, and in the last stages, the fine editor and finer colleague George Stroup. As I was preparing the book for publication, my research assistant Adam Copeland provided calm and competent support in tracking down obscure references and preparing the index. Thank you to the Louisville Institute, for funding my final year of dissertation research. To Iain Torrance, I offer my gratitude for reading the manuscript and encouraging its publication.

I need to say a special word of thanks to the congregation that allowed me to live and work in their midst, and who graciously agreed to be the case study for my research for chapter four. Members of this community patiently filled out surveys and in interviews shared with me powerful and intensely personal reflections on the Lord's Supper. The pastors welcomed my questions and observations, even when they were critical, and showed gracious forbearance with an eager young graduate student. I am grateful for the trust they have shown me, and I hope in my own account that I have shown them the honor they deserve.

Finally, I thank my family for their encouragement and unceasing support during the long years of gestation of this work. My father Walter Moore has been not only my teacher on the subtleties of medieval and Reformation theology, but my role model as a scholar who cares deeply about both academy and church. My mother has encouraged me with her unflagging good humor as well as her own careful editorial eye. My daughters Miriam and Fiona have shown impressive patience with their mother as she has tried (and failed) to attend faithfully to both scholarship and family. And to my faithful husband Chris, for sharing my passion for the eucharistic feast, and for being my partner in welcoming others to the table, my thanks can never be enough.

A Eucharistic Event

The Setting

First Presbyterian Church[1] is a large congregation in a small town in the southeastern part of the United States. Folks in this church tend to be well off, politically conservative, and white, and the majority are not originally from the area. The town's political powers are members here: mayor and town council members, publisher of the newspaper, owner of two major resorts, bankers, lawyers, doctors. Their children make up the large and active youth group as well as the swarm of younger children who toddle, crawl, and run to the front of the sanctuary for the children's sermon each week. These working professionals and their families worship side by side with retirees from up north, many of them former business executives or retired military officers. Members of the congregation are well dressed, and the parking lot — full of late-model SUVs, minivans, and Japanese cars — reveals a very comfortable standard of living.

The two clergy who serve in this church fit within the broad demographic portrait of the congregation: both are white males with wives and children, and though both come from the southeastern United States, neither comes from this area. The pastor is approaching 50, and his salary is comparable to the majority of the congregation. The associate is in his early 30s, politically to the left of most members of the congregation and with a salary lower than most.

---

1. Not the real name of this congregation.

The church buildings are large and well kept, taking up most of a block in a residential section of town near the old downtown area. The arrangement of buildings and parking areas means that there is no single route of access to the worship space. But though they approach by different routes, all enter the sanctuary from the large, well-lit, and formally furnished narthex.

Inside the sanctuary, the wooden pews are arranged in semi-circular auditorium style seating around the central raised pulpit area. There is also a large rear balcony, which provides about a third of the seating space in the building. Two large side windows provide good light for the interior on a sunny morning, but this natural light is supplemented by ornate chandeliers as well as dozens of lights in the ceiling. The main visual foci are a white and gilt cross suspended over the communion table, and exposed organ pipes framing a rose window in the upper part of the rear chancel wall. The forty-voice choir sits in the loft at the front of the sanctuary, behind and slightly above the clergy. The central pulpit area is surrounded by ample open space, regularly used for gathering elders to serve communion and gathering children for children's sermons, as well as accommodating weddings and funerals. In front of the dais on the floor sits the communion table, used for the offering plates on non-communion Sundays. On the dais itself, which is about five carpeted steps from the floor, are the pulpit on the left and font on the right, with the flower table between and against the rear railing.

To someone analyzing the seating arrangement, it appears that the communion table is the focal point of the worship space. One elder, looking at a diagram of the sanctuary, observed that the church was seated in a circle around the table. However, this is not the effect from the perspective of the pew. In practice, the table is not easily visible to everyone in the congregation, and other symbols are much more prominent: the suspended cross and stained-glass window — as well as the always-gorgeous flower arrangement, framed by lit candles at each worship service.

The Event

It is 11:45 on a Sunday morning in October. In the large sanctuary, about 400 people are gathered quietly, their attention focused on the black-robed minister at the pulpit. He has just completed his twelve-minute sermon, focusing on the "lunar communion service" celebrated by one church in Texas with the astronaut and Presbyterian elder Buzz Aldrin when he was on the moon. After a pause to let his final point sink in, the preacher breathes out, saying, "Let us pray." The congregation bows heads for a brief prayer, during which the dimmed lights come back up. The two ministers then descend the steps of the dais to stand behind the communion table, which sits on the floor.

The table itself has been specially prepared for the communion service. On a non-communion Sunday the table holds a rough ceramic plate and cup, along with the gold offering plates. Today, however, there are a small silver plate with a roll wrapped in a white napkin, a silver pitcher filled with grape juice, a matching silver chalice, two stacks of silver plates with small pre-cut squares of white bread, and two stacks of silver trays filled with plastic cups of Welch's grape juice. Speaking without script directly to the congregation, the pastor invites the people to table in a glad, insistent voice:

> This table, too, is a big table, welcoming not just Presbyterians, but all Christians, all believers, all baptized believers to partake of this meal — with brothers and sisters in Christ around this world and, at least one time, with a brother in Christ on the surface of the moon. It's a *big* table. And all baptized believers are welcome.

The pastor then gives a brief nod to the associate, who turns to the black notebook in his hand and begins the Great Prayer of Thanksgiving:

> Leader: The Lord be with you.
> *People: And also with you.*
> Leader: Lift up your hearts.
> *People: We lift them up to the Lord.*
> Leader: Let us give thanks to the Lord our God.
> *People: It is right to give our thanks and praise.*

Here most congregants close their eyes and settle into their seats to listen as the associate continues in his quiet, earnest voice:

3

PROLOGUE

Leader: Holy God, Father Almighty, Creator of heaven and earth, with joy we praise you and give thanks to your name. You formed the universe in your wisdom and created all things by your power. You set us in families of the earth to live with you in faith. We praise you for good gifts of bread and the cup, and for the table you spread in the world as a sign of your love for all people in Christ. Great and wonderful are your works, Lord God Almighty. Your ways are just and true. Therefore we lift our hearts in joyful praise, joining our voices with choirs of angels and with all the faithful in every time and place, who forever sing to the glory of your name:

At this point, the organist plays the introductory chords to the Sanctus while members of the congregation prepare to sing, some from memory, most from the hymnal. The singing is fairly robust, led by the well-trained choir:

All: *Holy, holy, holy Lord, God of power and might,*
Heaven and earth are full of your glory.
Hosanna in the highest.
Blessed is he who comes in the name of the Lord.
Hosanna in the highest, hosanna in the highest.

As the music fades, the associate minister moves on to remember the life, death, and resurrection of Jesus Christ:

Leader: We praise you, most holy God, for sending your Son to live among us, sharing our joy and sorrow. He told your story, healed the sick, and was a friend of sinners. Obeying you, he took up his cross and died that we might live. We praise you that he overcame death and is risen to rule the world. He is still the friend of sinners. We trust him to overcome every power that can hurt or divide us and believe that when he comes in glory, we will celebrate victory with him. Remembering all your mighty and merciful acts, we break bread and share one cup, giving thanks for your saving love in Jesus Christ. As you raised our Lord from death, and call us with him from death to life, we give ourselves to you and to live for him in joy and grateful praise. So we proclaim the mystery of faith:

Most worshipers recognize this last line as another cue, printed in the worship bulletin, and so they turn to read the next response as printed on the page:

> *All: Christ has died, Christ is risen, Christ will come again.*

And again the associate continues:

> Leader: Gracious God, pour out your Holy Spirit upon us and upon these gifts of bread and the cup. Make them be for us the body and blood of Christ that we may be for the world the body of Christ redeemed by his blood. Send us out in the power of the Spirit to live for others as Christ lived for us, announcing his death for the sins of the world and telling his resurrection to all people and nations. By your Holy Spirit, draw us together into one body and join us to Christ the Lord that we may remain his glad and faithful people until we feast with him in glory.
>
> Through Christ, with Christ, in Christ, in the unity of the Holy Spirit, all glory and honor are yours, almighty God, now and forever.

As he prays this final section, the associate makes a gesture of blessing over the elements with one hand, the other hand holding his book. Few, however, observe this action. While the minister is praying solo, most members of the congregation have their heads bowed and eyes closed, opening their eyes only in order to read (or sing) the responses. The prayer ends with a unison Lord's Prayer, which everyone recites from memory.

After the final "Amen," the people open their eyes and, after checking to see where they are in the order of worship, redirect their attention to the pastor at the table. Picking up the bread, he relates a version of the Words of Institution based on 1 Corinthians 11. When the text says "He took bread, and when he had given thanks, he broke it . . . ," he pauses and tears the loaf in two. So also when the text says, "Likewise also he took the cup, saying 'this is the new covenant in my blood' . . . ," he pours the juice from the pitcher into the chalice, holding it up for all to see. As with the invitation, these words he recites from memory, not adhering to one particular biblical translation but telling the familiar story to people who have heard it many times before. The worshipers, for their part, attend carefully to this portion of the service, their quiet focus signaling that this is the high point of communion for many. When the bread has been broken and juice poured, the pastor gestures to the serving elders, who come forward from their places in the congregation and stand facing the table. They fidget their way into a straight line, checking to make sure that they are in the right order. Most of these men and women are dressed in dark colors at the formal end of the congregation's range of attire. The two ministers pass out the trays of bread to them. As each elder receives a tray, she turns and walks down an aisle to her assigned place to begin serving.

Once the elders start moving, the organist begins to play the introduction to the first hymn to be sung during the distribution. This has not been the usual practice for this congregation; most folk are accustomed to soft organ music accompanying the distribution. As a result, the congregation is uncertain at this point; some sing, others listen to the choir and organ. Four hymns are listed in the worship bulletin; the organist plays through the first and then skips to the third ("Let Us Break Bread Together"). This confuses the congregation further; some begin singing the second hymn, others go to the third, others drop out altogether. The elders finish serving the bread and juice before it becomes necessary to move to the fourth hymn.

During the singing, the elders pass the plates down the pews, and each person takes a square of bread. Some eat it immediately, but most hold it for a few seconds before consuming it. Juggling hymnals and communion trays complicates the process for some people, especially the elderly members of the congregation. These folks tend to give up on the singing altogether until they have been served both bread and juice. Others manage to balance the two activities with grace, setting the hymnal on the pew to pass the tray and then resuming singing with the hymnal in hand after consuming the elements. There is no speaking, except for a few whispered logistical comments ("Have you got it?" "No, pass it the other way," or "thank you"). One of the elders silently serves the two ministers in their chairs on the dais. As each elder finishes serving her section of people, she proceeds to the back of the sanctuary, where the servers wait until all are reassembled. They then process down the aisle in double file to gather around the table.

The ministers retrieve the bread plates and pass out the trays of juice. The distribution of the juice proceeds as with the bread, but as each person finishes drinking, he places the empty cup in the holder designated for that purpose on the back of the pew in front of him. When the elders are once again assembled at the table after distributing all of the juice, the two ministers serve them communion, each minister serving half the elders bread, then juice. As they serve, the ministers say softly to these elders, "the body of Christ broken for you," and "the blood of Christ shed for you," but they speak too softly for the rest of the congregation to hear. Some of the elders respond with a smile, while others say "Amen." This verbal exchange is more intimate than any of the whispered negotiations between elders and congregational members, giving this portion of the communion service the feeling of an inner circle which is being observed — but not quite overheard — by the rest of the congregation.

After the elders are served and the music ends, the two ministers return to their places behind the table, and after straightening up the serving pieces, the associate minister turns to his book and prays:

> God of grace, you renew us at your table with the bread of life. May this meal strengthen us in love and help us to serve you in each other and in the world. We ask this in the name of Jesus Christ our Lord. Amen.

During the introduction to the hymn that follows, the elders return to their seats and both ministers return to their chairs on the dais.

The eucharistic portion of the service concludes at this point, although worship continues with a collection of the offering, singing of the doxology, prayer of thanksgiving, closing hymn, introduction of visitors, spoken benediction, and choral benediction.

This is a snapshot of one eucharistic event in the life of one local congregation. What is its theology?

INTRODUCTION

The Problem

Q. 168. What is the Lord's Supper?

    A. The Lord's Supper is a sacrament of the New Testament, wherein by giving and receiving bread and wine according to the appointment of Jesus Christ, his death is showed forth; and they that worthily communicate, feed upon his body and blood to their spiritual nourishment and growth in grace; have their union and communion with him confirmed; testify and renew their thankfulness and engagement to God, and their mutual love and fellowship each with other, as members of the same mystical body.[1]

This definition of the Lord's Supper, from the Westminster Catechism, is a summary of major themes in Reformed eucharistic theology. Here we have the emphasis on the sacrament's New Testament origins; the mention of both bread *and* wine as elements in the eucharist; the implication that the sacrament is effective only in those who "worthily communicate"; and finally, a list of the meanings of participation in the Lord's Supper: spiritual nourishment, confirmation of union with Christ, and testament to one's gratitude to God and mutual love with others present. It is a rich definition of the eucharist, born out of centuries of Christians celebrating the sacrament and reflecting on their

---

1. Westminster Larger Catechism, question 168, in *The Book of Confessions: Study Edition* (Louisville: Geneva Press, 1996), 7.278.

8

actions. It remains, however, a carefully constructed definition of right doctrine, with little attention to the details of eucharistic practice. We might call this theology *about* eucharist.

Contrast this catechism definition of the eucharist with the description in the prologue of a particular celebration of the sacrament in one local church. This is an ordinary celebration of the Lord's Supper in a large, affluent Southern Presbyterian congregation. An outside observer might notice that this ritual of bread and wine bears some resemblance to a meal, accompanied by music and framed by prayer. Indeed, if the observer listened attentively to the words of the minister, she would note the explicit connection between this ritual meal and a particular historical meal that took place long ago. The participants are solemn but not morose — clearly this is a serious but not funereal occasion. They do not interact with one another except to pass the trays of bread and juice down the row. The language of the prayers is formal, with ancient turns of phrase; one has the sense that this transaction has been practiced for a long time, and that the participants are aware of themselves as carrying on an ancient tradition.

An outside observer would notice these and many other details. Someone overhearing the thoughts of those present at this Lord's Supper would doubtless come away with a confused mass of reflections, but a few themes would emerge repeatedly: in this meal we remember the sacrifice of Jesus Christ; this bread and juice somehow unite us to Jesus Christ; Jesus Christ is the bread of life who sustains us. All of these details, those gleaned from the outside observer as well as those gathered by the overhearing observer, make up a theology — not a theology as neat and formal as Westminster, but a theology all the same. We might call this theology *of* or *emergent in* the eucharist.

What do these two descriptions of eucharist have to do with one another? They are obviously related. Westminster calls the Lord's Supper a "sacrament of the New Testament" in which bread and wine are given and received "according to the appointment of Jesus Christ"; in the local celebration Jesus' words from the New Testament are read, and bread and wine are given and received. The prayers of the minister have language about thankfulness and about mutual love, themes that appear in the catechism. But there is much more in the actual practice of eucharist than any catechism's theological definition can contain. What difference does it make, for instance, that the senior minister says the Words of Institution, while the associate minister leads all the prayers? What difference does it make that there is singing rather than instrumental music — or rather than silence — during the distribution of the elements? What kind of experience and understanding about God — and hence what kind of *theology* — do the ritual details evoke?

Too often we in the Reformed tradition have focused on doctrinal formulations, such as the one in the Westminster Catechism, as the starting points of eucharistic theology. We have regarded the eucharist as the enacting of carefully formed doctrines about Christ and church: here at the table we understand that Christ is really — but not corporeally — present and that in partaking of the bread and wine we are reminded of the meal Jesus shared with his disciples on the night when he was betrayed. We come to the table with these doctrines, and because we understand them properly, we can rightly partake of the sacrament. The focus shifts from encounter to interpretation. This view of the eucharist as the proper acting out of right doctrine stems from the usual interpretation of the reformers' intent with regard to liturgy in general. As historian Howard Hageman says, "Above all [the reformers] wanted their liturgy to be an adequate and accurate *expression* of their theology . . . the rediscovered theology of the Word of God."[2] Liturgy was to express a theology already formed. Brian Gerrish also unintentionally suggests this view when he says about Calvin's eucharistic theology, "The holy banquet is simply the liturgical *enactment* of the theme of grace and gratitude that lies at the heart of Calvin's entire theology."[3] The language of "enactment" can suggest that the ritual meal is a secondary acting out of a prior theology.

There is something right about this approach to the Lord's Supper. The sixteenth-century reformers were reacting against what they regarded as a total lack of understanding of the eucharist in the medieval church. Luther, Zwingli, and Calvin were all concerned to restore to the people a sense that the Words of Institution were not a magical incantation, but a recounting of the event on which salvation de-

---

2. Howard G. Hageman, *Pulpit and Table: Some Chapters in the History of Worship in the Reformed Churches* (Richmond: John Knox Press, 1962), pp. 14f., emphasis mine.

3. Brian Gerrish, *Grace and Gratitude: The Eucharistic Theology of John Calvin* (Minneapolis: Fortress Press, 1993), p. 20, emphasis mine.

pends. People needed to understand what they were doing so that they could rightly worship God, and not the elements of the eucharist.

There is something right about this approach to the Lord's Supper, but in and of itself it is insufficient. If we regard the celebration of the eucharist as simply a "liturgical enactment" of some externally formulated theological theme, then two things follow. First, we trivialize the power of ritual action. Ritual itself does not merely enact prior belief; it also forms beliefs. What we do impacts the way we think, and not just the other way around. This is why the reformers were so concerned about what they termed the abuses of the mass: Luther, Calvin, and others recognized the power of ritual action to shape worshipers' beliefs about God, humanity, and the world. The reformers worked so hard to alter liturgical practice because they knew that in changing practice, they would be changing theology. Second, this understanding of the liturgy as secondary to doctrine can lead to an idolatry of reason. When "doctrine" itself is construed narrowly as the propositional statement of truth claims,[4] and when such doctrine is then judged to be prior to liturgical action, there is a dangerous exaltation of reason over liturgical practice. As a practical result, the effectiveness of the eucharist is made dependent on our human understanding of it. An appropriate focus on theological understanding of the sacrament, intended to direct the worshipers' attention to God, can then slip into a preoccupation with understanding itself, which directs our attention to ourselves. It is ironic that Calvin's concern about idolatry of the sacrament, which prompted a vast quantity of theological reflection, has led some of his theological heirs to the opposite idolatry: the idolatry of reason itself. In this situation, the eucharist may cease to be the holy encounter of a community with God and instead may become an individual intellectual exercise.

Many things have made me aware of the problems in regarding the eucharist as merely enactment of prior doctrine. To begin with, after

4. This is one of the understandings of doctrine criticized by George Lindbeck: a propositional view that "emphasizes the cognitive aspects of religion and stresses the ways in which church doctrines function as informative propositions or truth claims about objective realities" (*The Nature of Doctrine: Religion and Theology in a Postliberal Age* [Philadelphia: Westminster Press, 1984], p. 16). It is particularly problematic to treat eucharistic doctrine in this manner, since this approach focuses on cognitive comprehension to the exclusion of lived, embodied practice.

college I lived for a year in India, as an outsider to a religious tradition that is saturated with ritual action. It was clear that, even for those minimally trained in Hindu teachings, the rituals of everyday life are enormously powerful, shaping the way people live and move and have their being in the world. This experience led me to reflect on my own religious tradition and its apparent lack of interest in ritual. Might it be the case that there, too, ritual could be a powerful influence in shaping and forming people? And might it even be the case that ritual has a place already in the Reformed tradition, but a place that has not been acknowledged or examined in recent years?

Secondly, readings in liturgical theology introduced me to the concept of liturgy as *primary theology* and formulated doctrine as *secondary theology*. I have alluded to this distinction above in calling the detailed description of eucharistic practice a theology *of* eucharist, while the catechism definition is theology *about* eucharist. According to liturgical theologians such as Gordon Lathrop, Aidan Kavanagh, and Don Saliers, all theology grows out of the liturgy and the liturgy itself is theology. This challenges the common Reformed view that liturgy follows theology. If liturgy is primary theology, then surely Reformed worship needs to be reexamined for the theology it creates, not simply for the doctrine it is supposed to enact.

Finally, reading performance theorists such as Charles Briggs, Ann Gold, and Gloria Raheja has alerted me to the principle of *emergence* in ritual performance. Like the liturgical theologians cited above, these performance theorists insist that meaning does not merely precede a particular ritual performance; meaning *emerges* in the midst of the performance. A ritual does not simply enact a fully formed myth, for example, but it presents the myth in a particular way that imbues it with new meaning in that local context.[5] So also, I have concluded, the eucharist in the Reformed tradition is more than the acting out of a set of beliefs or the recollection of a historical event; it is the site of emergent meaning that we can only grasp by attending to the particular details of local eucharistic performances.

All of these wide-ranging experiences and readings have led me back to the origins of the Reformed tradition, and especially to the writings of John Calvin. Do Calvin and other Reformed theologians

---

5. For a fuller discussion of this principle of emergence, see below, pp. 98ff.

provide resources to rethink the eucharist as more than the mere enactment of right doctrine? Does Calvin himself exhibit a respect for
the embodied, ritual dimension of the eucharist as something that not
only reflects, but also forms articulated theology? These questions
guide my discussion in chapter one. In chapter two, I turn to liturgical
theology for a model of doing theology that begins with practice, with
the liturgy. Here I explore some of the themes mentioned above, prob-
ing both the strengths and the weaknesses of current liturgical theologies when it comes to respect for actual local practice. In chapter three,
I examine some recent trends in ritual and performance theories, in
order to see how these anthropological approaches to ritual practice
might inform theology. In particular, recent ritual scholars focus attention on the local doing of ritual as an activity that generates meaning — an insight that sharpens my own focus on the local, the particular, in the doing of theology. Chapter four contains my attempt at
constructing a local eucharistic theology from the practices and reflections of one community of faith. Here I use tools drawn from the three
previous chapters. And in chapter five I suggest ways in which this
theological exercise might be instructive for future Reformed theology.

Throughout the project, my focus will be on eucharistic theology,
on a way of approaching eucharist through the practices of an actual
believing community. My larger goal, however, is to move toward a
way of doing theology that begins with the practices, with the "doing"
itself.[6]

---

6. In recent years, several scholars have begun to engage in serious conversation
about the deep interconnections between theology and practices. These include
Reinhard Hütter, *Suffering Divine Things: Theology as Church Practice* (Grand Rapids:
Eerdmans, 1999); James J. Buckley and David S. Yeago, eds., *Knowing the Triune God:
The Work of the Spirit in the Practices of the Church* (Grand Rapids: Eerdmans, 2001); and
Miroslav Volf and Dorothy C. Bass, eds., *Practicing Theology: Beliefs and Practices in
Christian Life* (Grand Rapids: Eerdmans, 2002). I intend my own project to contribute
in a small way to this emerging conversation.

CHAPTER 1

Struggling for Balance:
John Calvin and the Reformed Tradition

The Reformed tendency to regard doctrine as prior to liturgical practice can be traced back to the sixteenth-century Reformation. At that time, concern about abuses in the medieval Roman Catholic mass led many reformers to engage in bitter debate about the proper meaning of the eucharist. Beginning with Luther, all the magisterial reformers agreed that the notion of transubstantiation, the actual transformation of the substance of the bread into the body of Christ at consecration, was a false doctrine. It had supported an array of medieval devotional practices which the reformers found abhorrent: adoration of the host as the focal point of the mass, processions of the consecrated host through the streets, the feast of Corpus Christi. These practices were idolatry, claimed the reformers. Such ritual actions directed attention to the material object rather than to God. But although the reformers agreed that transubstantiation was wrong, they could not agree on which interpretation was correct. Indeed, the different understandings of the eucharist contributed in large part to the divisions among Protestants: Lutheran, Reformed, Anabaptist. Each Protestant camp came to defend its own interpretation of the eucharist so strongly that right interpretation became the precondition for participation in communion.

Historian Edward Muir regards this shift in eucharistic emphasis — from holy encounter to hermeneutical act — as illustrative of a larger shift in ritual theory in sixteenth-century Europe, from doing to meaning.[1] The primary question about a ritual shifted from "What does it

1. Edward Muir, *Ritual in Early Modern Europe* (Cambridge: Cambridge University Press, 1997). I will discuss this argument further in chapter three below.

do?" to "What does it *mean*?" Although Muir decries this hermeneutical emphasis in ritual as the divisive legacy of the Reformation, it is important to pause and recognize why the reformers were so passionate about proper understanding of meaning. I hope to show that at least for John Calvin, the concern about right understanding did not eclipse attention to the ritual event itself. In fact, his concern about proper understanding was prompted by a concern that people participate more fully in worship. Focus on doctrinal formulation was not to the detriment of, but in service of, worship of God. In particular, Calvin understood the eucharist as an event through which the Holy Spirit works to shape people over time into relationships with one another and with God's own self. This is a view of eucharist which was muted in some subsequent Reformed theologians, but which can be helpfully retrieved today.

Calvin himself was a second-generation reformer, and in his eucharistic theology he attempted to steer a middle course between two major Protestant reformers who had preceded him: Martin Luther and the first-generation Reformed leader, Ulrich Zwingli. In order to appreciate Calvin's own position, we must briefly examine the eucharistic debate between these two theologians.

Luther and Zwingli

Luther, while rejecting the Roman Catholic teaching on transubstantiation, continued to assert that Christ was really present "in, with, and under" the elements of the eucharist, a view that has come to be known as consubstantiation. Zwingli, on the other hand, understood the Lord's Supper primarily as a "memorial meal," an act by which the community of faith remembered the gift of Jesus Christ and attested their allegiance to God. Between 1526 and 1529, the two reformers attacked each other's eucharistic theologies through hostile pamphlets. In 1529, however, the threats of Emperor Charles V against the Protestants prompted an effort to unify the Protestant principalities of Germany and Switzerland against the incursions of the emperor. This situation led to the historic meeting of the two reformers which has come to be known as the Marburg Colloquy.[2]

2. For historical background, see Timothy George, *Theology of the Reformers* (Nash-

In 1529, at the invitation of Philip of Hesse, one of the Protestant princes, Luther and Zwingli met at Philip's castle in Marburg to try and agree upon a common theological platform.[3] According to the reports, Luther wrote the words *"Hoc est corpus meum"* on the table in front of him at the beginning of the colloquy, and the interpretation of this sentence guided much of the debate.[4] Luther understood this as a literal claim: the bread *is* Christ's body, in some mysterious way that we cannot comprehend. We must trust this to be true because Christ said it, and there is nothing in the biblical text to mitigate its literal reality.

Zwingli countered Luther by arguing that this was a figurative statement, just as there are many passages in the Bible that we understand to be figurative. As Zwingli's colleague Oecolampadius argued,

> The Holy Scriptures frequently employ figurative speech, metaphors, metonymies, and the like. In such cases words have a meaning different from what they say. Thus the words "This is my body" may also be figurative speech, as in the expressions: "John is Elijah" (Matt. 11:14); "The rock was Christ" (I Cor. 10:4); "I am the true vine" (John 15:1); "The seed is the Word of God" (Luke 8:11).[5]

"Is" here means "signifies"; it points to something beyond itself. Surely God would not order us to eat his flesh bodily. "The soul 'eats' spirit, and therefore it does not eat flesh," said Zwingli.[6] He frequently backed up his arguments with his favored text, John 6:63: "It is the

---

ville: Broadman Press, 1988), pp. 148-50 and Steven Ozment, *The Age of Reform 1250-1550: An Intellectual and Religious History of Late Medieval and Reformation Europe* (New Haven: Yale University Press, 1980), pp. 334-37.

3. For a brief account of this meeting, see George, *Theology of the Reformers*, pp. 148-54. For the most complete English reconstruction of the colloquy from the sources, see Herman Sasse, *This Is My Body: Luther's Contention for the Real Presence in the Sacrament of the Altar* (Minneapolis: Augsburg Publishing House, 1959), pp. 223-68. See also Donald J. Ziegler, ed., *Great Debates of the Reformation* (New York: Random House, 1969), pp. 71-107, which provides an English translation of Walter Koehler's German reconstruction of Marburg. The Latin and German original sources are available in the Weimar edition of Luther's works: *WA* 30, III, 110-59.

4. Sasse, *This Is My Body,* p. 232.

5. Sasse, *This Is My Body,* p. 232.

6. Sasse, *This Is My Body,* p. 239.

spirit that gives life, the flesh is of no avail." Sacramental eating is by faith, not by mouth. Salvation comes as a direct gift of the Holy Spirit, and does not depend on externals.

Luther protested that we cannot do away with external things, because God has ordained that "forgiveness of sins, eternal life, and the kingdom of heaven are, by the Word of God, attached to these low and, as it would seem, carnal things."[7] To be sure, the Lord's Supper is a symbol, signifying salvation, but it is a symbol that contains what it symbolizes.

> I pick up a wooden or silver rose and ask: what is this? You answer: it is a rose. For I did not ask about its meaning, but about its being, so you told me what it was, not what it signified . . . "Is" always has to do with being. There is no other way to take it. But you say: it is not a rose, it is a piece of wood. Well, I answer, all right. But it is still a rose. Even if it is not a natural, organic rose out of my garden, it is still essentially a rose, in its own way. There are lots of roses — silver ones, gold ones, cloth, paper, stone, wooden. Nonetheless, each is in its own way, and essentially, a rose in its being. Not just a mere sign. Why, how could there be any *signifying* unless there were first a *being*? Whatever *is* nothing *signifies* nothing. Whatever signifies first has to be, and to be like that other thing.[8]

Being precedes meaning. Luther argued here that just as the silver or wooden rose is still really a rose, so also the eucharistic elements are really the body and blood of Christ. He used the language of "essence" rather than "substance," to avoid the problems he saw in the doctrine of transubstantiation. Christ's presence cannot be circumscribed in a "mathematical way," but he is still present according to the Word of God.[9] The efficacy of the sacrament depends on God's words, not on

7. Sasse, *This Is My Body,* p. 234.

8. WA 26, 383, 22-35, as translated in H. G. Haile, *Luther: An Experiment in Biography* (New York: Doubleday, 1980), pp. 126-27.

9. "Let us not try to inquire *how* Christ's body is in the Lord's Supper. In Holy Scripture I do not admit mathematical dimensions. *God is higher than all mathematicians.* Christ can keep his body without space at a certain place. *He is in the sacrament (but) not as in a place.*" Sasse, *This Is My Body,* p. 255. Italics in Sasse.

human faith, according to Luther.[10] Thus his emphasis was on the objectivity of the gift in the Supper.

Zwingli responded to Luther's argument by saying, "We, too, speak of a sacramental presence of the body of Christ, which means that the body of Christ is in the Supper representatively."[11] Christ could not be literally present in the elements because of the distinction between his divine and human natures; since the ascension, Christ's physical body has been in heaven.[12] We do not unite with him physically in the eucharist. Rather, at the Lord's Supper the community of faith pledges their allegiance to Christ.[13] Zwingli's emphasis was on the faith of the believers which was publicly professed at communion.

Calvin: Attempting to Find a Balance

Calvin attempted to steer between these two theological positions, neither completely affirming nor completely rejecting Luther or Zwingli. Early in his section on the Lord's Supper in the *Institutes,* he lists two "faults" to guard against: "too little regard for signs, thus divorcing them from their mysteries, and too much regard for signs, thus obscuring the mysteries themselves."[14] The first fault is that of Zwingli, the second, that of Luther. Calvin always sought to balance

10. Sasse, *This Is My Body,* p. 246.

11. Sasse, *This Is My Body,* p. 256.

12. As Timothy George points out, Luther's emphasis on the unity of Christ's natures more closely resembles the Monophysite argument, while Zwingli stands closer to the Nestorian position with his emphasis on the distinction between Christ's humanity and divinity. (See George, *Theology of the Reformers* p. 153.) According to Luther, Christ could be literally present in the elements because of the "ubiquity of the body." Calvin objects to this Lutheran point, arguing like Zwingli that Christ's body exists now in heaven, which is why it is not brought down to unite with the elements, but we are taken up to unite with him. See Calvin, *Institutes of the Christian Religion,* ed. John T. McNeill, trans. Ford Lewis Battles, Library of Christian Classics, vols. XX-XXI (Philadelphia: Westminster Press, 1960), 4.17.26-31. Hereafter cited as *Institutes.*

13. See George, *Theology of the Reformers,* p. 158. Two centuries later, Jonathan Edwards used a similar image to describe the Lord's Supper: "The Lord's Supper is a mutual solemn profession of two parties transacting the covenant of grace" ("Inquiry Concerning Qualifications for Communion," in *The Works of Jonathan Edwards,* vol. 1 [Edinburgh: Banner of Truth Trust, 1974], II.9, p. 458).

14. *Institutes* 4.17.5.

respect for the "signs," the embodied reality of the eucharistic event, and respect for the "mysteries," that is, the living Christ who cannot be contained in the event. His concern for right meaning, for doctrine, emerges when either of these faults is evident.[15]

In turning attention to Calvin's eucharistic theology, I do not mean to imply that his is the only Reformed theological voice worth hearing. Zwingli as well as others — Bucer, Bullinger, and Oecolampadius, to name a few — made significant contributions to Reformed theology in the sixteenth century and continue to merit attention today. I focus on Calvin's contribution for two reasons: first, because Calvin has exercised a pervasive influence on the development of the Reformed tradition; and second, because, curiously, his influence on the Reformed understanding of the Lord's Supper has not been particularly strong until recently. It is out of respect for his historic significance as well as his fruitful but overlooked contribution to the issue at hand that leads me to call attention to him here.

Calvin's concern about proper understanding of the eucharist has led some scholars of Protestant liturgy to criticize him and his successors for a tendency toward didacticism in liturgical practice. James White, for instance, comments, "So great was the imperative to teach that each service contains a condensed course in theology and ethics. This became a lasting characteristic of Reformed worship, contributing to its overwhelmingly cerebral character."[16] To be sure, a didactic tone has haunted the Reformed liturgical tradition from the beginning. In the eucharistic liturgy he developed for Strasbourg and Geneva, Calvin led up to the distribution of the elements with a series of safeguards against misinterpretation of the ritual action.[17]

---

15. Much of the following discussion of Calvin is indebted to the work of B. A. Gerrish in his volume *Grace and Gratitude: The Eucharistic Theology of John Calvin* (Minneapolis: Fortress Press, 1993). For a fascinating exploration of the connection between Calvin's eucharistic theology and new understandings of political and social power in the sixteenth century, see Christopher Elwood, *The Body Broken: The Calvinist Doctrine of the Eucharist and the Symbolization of Power in Sixteenth-Century France* (New York: Oxford University Press, 1999).

16. James F. White, *Protestant Worship: Traditions in Transition* (Louisville: Westminster/John Knox Press, 1989), p. 65. See also Joseph D. Small, "A Church of the Word and Sacrament," in *Christian Worship in Reformed Churches Past and Present*, ed. Lukas Vischer (Grand Rapids: Eerdmans, 2003), pp. 314-15.

17. See John Calvin, "The Form of Church Prayers and Hymns with the Manner of

Before the worshipers could approach the table, the minister was to explain who is eligible to participate, what constitutes faithful participation, and what participants are to understand by their actions. In particular, the lengthy exhortation preceding the distribution of the elements sounds ponderous to contemporary ears, going to great lengths to explain the ritual that is about to take place. One portion of this exhortation reads:

> . . . we may be conscious of much frailty and misery in ourselves, such that we do not have perfect faith, but are inclined toward defiance and unbelief, or that we do not devote ourselves fully to the service of God and with such zeal as we ought, but have to fight daily against the lusts of our flesh. Nevertheless, since our Lord has granted us the grace of having his gospel graven on our hearts, so that we may withstand all unbelief, and has given us the desire and longing to renounce our own wishes, that we may follow His righteousness and His holy commandments: let us be assured that the sins and imperfections which remain in us will not prevent Him from receiving us and making us worthy participants of this spiritual Table.[18]

To our ears, this can sound more like a theological treatise than a portion of eucharistic liturgy. And such a tone has contributed to the perception that Calvin and Calvinist liturgy are more interested in right doctrine than in right practice. But we must not be too hasty in judging this liturgy as merely "cerebral." Calvin, like all the sixteenth-century reformers, saw a tremendous need to educate the laity about what they were doing in worship, since so many theological misconceptions had grown up around the celebration of the mass. He was concerned about teaching, not because he wanted to form doctrinal positions, but because he wanted to form people into more faithful worshipers. Calvin, following the lead of Paul in 1 Corinthians, exhorted the congregation to self-examination so that they would ap-

---

Administering the Sacraments and Consecrating Marriage According to the Custom of the Ancient Church" (Strasbourg, 1545 and Geneva, 1542), in Bard Thompson, *Liturgies of the Western Church* (Cleveland: William Collins and World Publishing Co., 1961), pp. 197-208. Hereafter cited as "Form of Church Prayers."

18. "Form of Church Prayers," p. 206.

proach the table ready to be transformed by God's gift of grace there. In other words, though the sixteenth-century rhetoric may not be melodious to twenty-first-century ears, we should acknowledge that Calvin's intention was to move his congregation to more lively and engaged participation.[19]

A didactic tone in liturgy is part of the Reformed legacy, but we must understand it as only a part of Calvin's approach to liturgy in general and the eucharist in particular. On the one hand, Calvin worried about human misuse of ritual action; he was aware that embodied practices can exhibit a power that is demonic rather than divine. This led to his concern for explanation so that people may rightly participate in worship. But on the other hand, it is also clear that Calvin held sacramental activity in high esteem, as ritual practice ordained by God, through which the Holy Spirit works to gather people of faith to the risen Christ. Far from being a secondary expression of a doctrinal position, eucharistic practice is a primary event through which people encounter God.

Eucharist as primary formative event of encounter with God: this is the overarching theme that I want to retrieve from Calvin. And how does the eucharist form participants, according to this reformer? By appealing to them as fully embodied persons, heart, mind, ear, and mouth; that is to say, the Lord's Supper works precisely because it is not only aural reception of doctrine, but also oral reception of bread and wine. As Calvin emphasized, in the Supper, God has graciously condescended to communicate with our full humanity through both Word and sacrament.

Word and Sacrament

Word and sacrament are, according to Calvin, the two primary ways in which God communicates with humanity. Following Luther, Calvin calls Word and sacraments the "marks of the church."[20] Both are pres-

19. I am indebted to Stan Hall for this point. For a helpful brief discussion of the medieval sacramental system against which the reformers were reacting, see Elsie Anne McKee, "Reformed Worship in the Sixteenth Century," in *Christian Worship in Reformed Churches Past and Present*, ed. Lukas Vischer (Grand Rapids: Eerdmans, 2003), pp. 6-8.

20. See *Institutes* 4.1.9. For additional references to Word and sacrament as "marks of

ent in the celebration of the eucharist. Most of the time, Calvin insisted that Word and sacrament are mutually informing, the two primary means by which the Spirit unites humanity with Christ and with one another. But the relationship of Word and sacrament is complicated by the fact that Calvin used both "Word" and "sacrament" in more than one way. Reformed theologians since Calvin's time have disagreed about how to interpret his use of "Word," and particularly how to understand the relationship between Christ as Word and scripture as Word.[21]

As his use of "Word" varied, so also did Calvin's use of the term "sacrament." Sometimes he used this in a narrow sense, to refer to the concrete symbols of bread and wine as well as the actions performed with them. In this narrow sense, "sacrament" is the partner of "words." At other times, sacrament has a broader sense, referring to the eucharist as a whole, which includes both symbols and words.[22]

---

the church" or *notae ecclesiae,* see the Scots Confession 3.18 and Second Helvetic Confession 5.134-35 in *Book of Confessions: Study Edition* (Louisville: Geneva Press, 1996)

21. Calvin himself does not directly address more modern concerns about whether scripture itself is Word or human words that witness to the Word. One helpful lens, however, for interpreting Calvin's use of "Word" comes from the later Reformed theologian Karl Barth, who discusses the "threefold form of the Word of God." According to Barth, the Word is first and foremost Jesus Christ the Word revealed, secondarily the Word written in the words of scripture, and thirdly, the Word preached in human words. See Karl Barth, *Church Dogmatics* I.1: *The Doctrine of the Word of God,* trans. G. W. Bromiley and T. F. Torrance (Edinburgh: T. & T. Clark, 1975), par. 4, pp. 88-124. Barth himself was influenced by Heinrich Bullinger's discussion of scripture and preaching as Word of God in chapter 1 of the Second Helvetic Confession. See *Book of Confessions: Study Edition,* 5.001-5.004. These three forms are all the Word of God. But while the revealed Word is the first form of the Word, the basis of the other two, it comes to us today primarily through scripture and proclamation. Although Calvin himself never described the Word as threefold, Barth's discussion of "Word" here generally reflects Calvin's use of the term, for sometimes he used "Word" to refer to scripture, sometimes to proclamation, and other times more directly to Jesus Christ, the Word revealed. So at times in his eucharistic discussions, he exalted the Word, meaning the risen Christ, as that which precedes any particular sacramental act. At other times, he emphasized Word and sacrament as equal partners in communicating God to humanity. In these discussions, proclaimed words are intended to refer to the Word, but they are not identical with the risen Christ. For further discussion of Calvin's nuanced use of "Word," see Gerrish, *Grace and Gratitude,* pp. 76-86.

22. I am not using "sign" and "symbol" here in any contemporary technical sense,

Examples may clarify this complex relationship of Word and sacrament in Calvin's writing. Calvin did at times relegate sacramental objects to secondary status in relation to the Word. One instance of this is in his discussion of the *sursum corda*, the first part of the dialogue preceding the Great Prayer of Thanksgiving, which appears in the eucharist described in the prologue. In the *sursum corda*, the minister urges the people to lift their hearts from earthly to heavenly things:

> . . . let us lift our spirits and hearts on high where Jesus Christ is in the glory of His Father, whence we expect Him at our redemption. Let us not be fascinated by these earthly and corruptible elements which we see with our eyes and touch with our hands, seeking Him there as though He were enclosed in the bread or wine. Then only shall our souls be disposed to be nourished and vivified by His substance when they are lifted up above all earthly things, attaining even to heaven, and entering the Kingdom of God where He dwells. Therefore let us be content to have the bread and wine as signs and witnesses, seeking the truth spiritually where the Word of God promises that we shall find it.[23]

"Word of God" in this case refers to the risen Christ as attested in scripture and proclamation, while the sacramental objects are the material elements narrowly defined. Here Calvin was clearly struggling against the idolatry of the material elements which he saw in the mass. He was also implicitly indicting the Lutheran view that the body of Christ is to be found "in, with, and under" the bread and wine. In response, he urged people to focus on Jesus Christ in heaven rather than "earthly and corruptible elements," understanding that it is the Holy Spirit that lifts up our spirits to be in the presence of Christ. He expressed a similar sentiment in the "Short Treatise on the Lord's Supper," where he listed as one of the errors corrupting the sacrament the "carnal adoration of the bread." Rather than focusing on the visible

---

but in an attempt to reflect Calvin's own language. Calvin tended to use "sign" to refer to the material elements of bread and wine, while "symbol" had a fuller range of meaning: sometimes it was equivalent to "sign," but at other points it included material elements, accompanying gestures, and multivalent references.

23. "Form of Church Prayers," p. 207.

sign, we should adore Jesus Christ, said Calvin.[24] Again, he was trying here to combat the idolatry that he perceived in the medieval mass. But the effect of his effort, Bard Thompson suggests, is that the signs are used "in an incongruous way. . . . These creatures of *earth*, these signs of God's redemptive *condescension* were supposed to transport the believer *above* the material realm, to the Risen Lord in the far reaches of heaven."[25] By emphasizing the distance between Jesus Christ and the material signs, Thompson contends, Calvin rendered questionable the practice of the sacrament itself; for if Jesus Christ is to be sought in heaven rather than through these elements, why participate in this ritual?

But Calvin will not be dismissed so quickly. It may be that the words of the *sursum corda* appear to devalue the material elements in favor of a spiritual union with Christ, who cannot be seen. But to understand "spiritual union" with Christ as something utterly separate from the sacramental event is to misunderstand Calvin's eucharistic theology. According to Calvin, the Holy Spirit truly unites the faithful with Christ at the Lord's Supper; this does not detract from the sacrament, but leads to gratitude for the Spirit's gracious work in and through these material signs to join us to the ascended Christ. Calvin's emphasis on the "spiritual real presence" of Christ tries to avoid confusion of Christ's body with the material elements of bread and wine, but it is not therefore less "real." It is through the particular work of

24. Calvin, "Short Treatise on the Lord's Supper" (1541), in *Calvin: Theological Treatises,* trans. and ed. J. K. S. Reid, Library of Christian Classics, vol. XXII (Philadelphia: Westminster, 1954), p. 159. Hereafter cited as "Short Treatise on the Lord's Supper."

25. Bard Thompson, *Liturgies of the Western Church,* p. 187. On this theme, see also Ronald Wallace, *Calvin's Doctrine of the Word and Sacrament* (Edinburgh: Oliver & Boyd, 1953), p. 227, as well as Calvin's commentaries on Isaiah 37:16 and 40:20 and Acts 2:22. See Calvin, *Commentaries,* trans. and ed. Joseph Haroutunian and Louise Pettibone Smith, Library of Christian Classics, vol. XXIII (Philadelphia: Westminster, 1958), pp. 94, 121-22, 223-24. Kilian McDonnell also critiques Calvin for this distance between Jesus Christ and the material elements of the eucharist: "Does not the distinction to the point of opposition between the divinity and the humanity in Christ, and between the sign and the signified in the Eucharist make it extremely difficult to arrive at any real theological synthesis according to the law of the Incarnation?" (*John Calvin, the Church, and the Eucharist* [Princeton: Princeton University Press, 1967], p. 368).

the Spirit that Christ is present in the sacrament. We will return to this point later.

The *sursum corda* itself, even as it draws attention away from "these earthly and corruptible elements," is a ritual element that Calvin prescribed as the antidote to false understanding of the eucharist. By hearing the words "let us lift our spirits and hearts on high . . ." the worshipers should be led to understand that the elements themselves are not to be worshiped, but only Christ, the revealed Word of God. So this ritual element, even as its words devalue the material signs, depends on the presence of those signs to make its point. And further, it is intended to provoke a particular attitude in the worshiper: the raising of attention to heaven to be united with Christ. The sacrament as a whole is not being devalued here, but only a narrow construal of the sacrament as the material elements alone, as sign rather than more expansive symbol.

More problematic are those cases when Calvin suggested that the sacrament is not only subordinate to the Word as risen Christ, but subordinate to doctrine. In his "Short Treatise on the Lord's Supper," his clearest statement of eucharistic theology, he said, "The chief thing which our Lord recommends to us, is to celebrate this mystery with true intelligence. It follows then that the substance of it all consists in the doctrine."[26] He went on to say that because Jesus Christ has revealed doctrine so clearly to us, we have less need for symbols than did the people of the Old Testament. The purpose of ritual action, he implied here, is to communicate doctrine. If it does not do this, then it is at best useless, and at worst, downright dangerous. This is Calvin at his most polemical, insisting that the symbols themselves do not convey grace without a proper approach to the symbols, which is facilitated by right understanding.

He voiced a similar sentiment in his commentary on Hebrews when he said, "We see that the symbol was added after the law was explained: for what is a sacrament unless the Word come before it? Therefore the symbol is an *accessory* to the Word."[27] The sense of "Word" here is multivalent; it is certainly the revealed Word of God which precedes any particular sacramental celebration, but it also has

26. "Short Treatise on the Lord's Supper," p. 161.
27. Calvin, Commentary on Hebrews 9:18-20, in Calvin, *Commentaries*, p. 101. Emphasis mine.

practical implications: What is the point of a sacrament without the Word proclaimed before it? It is this practical implication that has presented problems for the Reformed tradition, because it suggests that sacramental practice is secondary to — not an equal partner with — the Word proclaimed. The Word precedes the sacrament and governs it; the symbol of the sacrament is secondary — an "accessory" — to the spoken word. It is this view that Ronald Wallace refers to when he notes that Calvin "puts sacraments in the strictly subordinate position to the word which the visible element in the Old Testament revelation has to the word spoken alongside it."[28] The Word has priority over the visible symbol here, just as, in the preceding example, the doctrine has priority over the practice.

It is important to understand that the passages denigrating symbol and exalting the Word are responding to the particular ritual abuses Calvin perceived in the medieval Roman Catholic mass. Despite these polemical outbursts against idolatry of the elements, Calvin did not usually see the proclaimed and written Word as more important than the sacrament but saw the two as requiring and mutually informing one another. Even in the commentary on Hebrews, where he called the symbol an "accessory" to the Word, he went on to balance his tirade against ritual abuse with the following words:

> . . . we receive God's promises only when they are confirmed by the blood of Christ . . . we hear God speaking to us only when we see Christ offering himself as a pledge in what is said to us. If we could only get it into our heads that the Word of God we read is written not so much with ink as with the blood of the Son of God.[29]

This passage makes it clear that for Calvin, the written Word of God we read was inextricably bound up with the sacramental idea of Christ's blood. Not only does the sacrament depend on the Word, but the Word also depends on the sacrament, for we need to see as well as hear in order to "receive God's promises." Even Wallace acknowledges this interdependence, saying "Though the sacraments are ineffective

28. Wallace, *Calvin's Doctrine*, p. 73.
29. Commentary on Hebrews, in Calvin, *Commentaries*, p. 101.

without the Word, nevertheless the bare word cannot have its full effect without the sacraments."[30] Word needs sacrament and sacrament needs Word. Neither can stand alone.[31]

This brings us to the mutual dependence of Word and sacrament, which most often characterizes Calvin's perspective. In this context, "Word" refers primarily to scripture and proclamation. According to Calvin, our human nature requires both visible and tangible symbols and audible words to come to true knowledge of God. In his initial discussion of sacraments in the *Institutes,* he explained that because of our ignorance, we have words, and because of our weakness, we have sacraments. Our faith is so weak that we need the earthly elements by which God unites us with God's own self.[32] Unflattering though this description may be, it does take seriously the human need for "earthly elements" to mediate the divine to humanity. Similarly, in his commentary on John 5:37, he claimed that God "puts on a visible form in the sacraments, so that he may be known by us *according to our own measure.*"[33] And in his commentary on Psalm 24, Calvin marveled, "It is a sign of the inestimable grace of God toward us . . . when, *due to the weakness of our flesh,* he lifts us up to himself by way of godly practices. For what is the purpose of the preaching of the Word, of the sacraments, of religious gatherings, and of the whole external order of the church except to unite us with God?"[34] Later in the commentary, he even went so far as to say "The preaching of the Word and the sacraments unite us with God. Therefore, we ought to hold on to these props with reverence, for if we spurn them in ungodly arrogance, it cannot be but that God shall remove himself far from us."[35] This passage shows how strongly Calvin felt about the place of external practices in the church; to go without these things was to risk being separated from God!

---

30. Wallace, *Calvin's Doctrine,* p. 137.

31. For more discussion on the unity of Word and sacrament, see Ron Byars, *Christian Worship: Glorifying and Enjoying God* (Louisville: Geneva Press, 2000), esp. pp. 38-41, and Joseph D. Small, "A Church of the Word and Sacrament," pp. 311-23.

32. *Institutes* 4.14.3. For a similar statement, see Calvin, "Short Treatise on the Lord's Supper," p. 144. See also Wallace, *Calvin's Doctrine,* p. 138.

33. Commentary on John 5:37, in Calvin, *Commentaries,* p. 400. Emphasis mine.

34. Commentary on Psalm 24, in Calvin, *Commentaries,* p. 393. Emphasis mine.

35. Commentary on Psalm 24, in Calvin, *Commentaries,* p. 394.

This emphasis on humanity's need for both sacraments *and* Word stands as a critique of much Protestant anthropology, which has focused on the Word to the exclusion of the sacraments. As James White points out,

> Protestantism has tended to neglect humanity's need for the visible and tangible. . . . We have, instead, settled for a lopsided anthropology, as if words were somehow more spiritual than actions. Who can say that Christ's self-giving through bread and wine is any less real than through the words of the sermon?[36]

Calvin recognized the human need for the "visible and tangible" as well as the audible. This is why he argued for frequent, even weekly, communion in Geneva: he understood that people regularly need the concrete partaking of bread and wine, in addition to the Word preached, to mediate the presence of God to them.[37]

This theological anthropology, which attends to the human need for comprehensible words *and* to the need for concrete symbols, is crucial for a reconsideration of the eucharist as a ritual event in which God acts, rather than as a merely human enactment of doctrine. Although Calvin implied that our need for the visible and tangible is a symptom of humanity's fallen condition, we do not have to agree with his negative judgment in order to affirm with him this fact of human nature as we know it. If humans require visible and tangible symbols, and if God has taken this into consideration and accommodated the divine presence to the material realm, then surely it is right for us to consider these visible and tangible elements when examining the eucharist. In other words, this anthropology provides a warrant for regarding the eucharist as an event in which God is involved with concrete symbols and spoken words, not only with extra-liturgical articulation of doctrine.

In his discussion of the eucharist in the *Institutes,* Calvin's balance of Word and sacrament, or word and embodied symbol, is clear. He in-

---

36. James F. White, *Sacraments as God's Self-Giving: Sacramental Practice and Faith* (Nashville: Abingdon Press, 1983), p. 25.

37. For a discussion of the importance of frequent communion, see "Short Treatise on the Lord's Supper," p. 153.

sisted that the eucharistic bread remains bread, even after the Words of Institution have been read. He emphasized that in order for people to understand that Christ's body is truly food for us, they must consider the purpose of the actual bread, which is truly food for our bodies. He therefore criticized the doctrine of transubstantiation, in which the substance of the bread is annihilated and Christ "hides under the figure."[38] The substance of the bread is integral to the meaning of the eucharist. So, as this instance illustrates, Calvin insisted on the integrity of the ritual object: namely, the eucharistic bread. This demonstrates his attempt to find the middle way between Luther and Zwingli; like Luther, he insisted that the physical symbol is indispensable, but like Zwingli, he did not identify the symbol with Christ's substantial presence.

Likewise Calvin sought the middle way with regard to actions: a physical action alone is not sufficient to accomplish the purpose of the ritual, but actions do have a kind of power. For instance, if those who are unworthy partake of the bread and wine of communion, they bring condemnation on themselves. Their action proclaims that salvation is only in Christ, but they lack the faith in this proclamation. Therefore, through their actions, "they are their own accusers."[39] Furthermore, Calvin showed his concern for proper actions in the eucharist by devoting eight subheadings of the *Institutes* to the details of celebration of the Lord's Supper.[40] Physical symbols, both objects and actions, are central to the eucharistic ritual.

But he also insisted that the physical symbols alone do not convey the whole truth. He declared that we must not "stop at the symbol" of the eucharistic elements, supposing Christ to reside there, but by the Holy Spirit, we must raise our minds to Christ in order to be united with him.[41] For "[i]f the function of the sacrament is to help the otherwise weak mind of man so that it may rise up to look upon the height of spiritual mysteries, then those who are halted at the outward sign wander from the right way of seeking Christ."[42] This is the function of

---

38. *Institutes* 4.17.14. On this same theme, see also "Short Treatise on the Lord's Supper," p. 157.

39. *Institutes* 4.17.40.

40. *Institutes* 4.17.43-50.

41. *Institutes* 4.17.29.

42. *Institutes* 4.17.36.

the *sursum corda*, according to Calvin: it is to raise the minds of the worshipers from the material elements to the heavenly body of Christ. Of course, the words themselves do not magically accomplish this, but in and through the words, the Holy Spirit works to turn the worshipers' attention to Christ in heaven so that they may be united with him. Here Calvin stressed the important role of words in the eucharistic ritual to clarify what is going on and to prompt the appropriate intention in the worshipers.

Words are a crucial element in the eucharistic ritual. Perhaps he overemphasized words as a reaction to the mass, but he was supremely concerned that people understand what they are doing. The ritual is not effective if they cannot hear the words or understand the language in which they are spoken. As he stated, "the Word must explain the sign" and "the sacrament requires preaching to beget faith."[43] The sacrament must include comprehensible words, because it is not the elements that are converted; people are converted.[44] This view of the converting power of words can be seen in his plea: "Let us understand that these words are living preaching which edifies its hearers, penetrates into their very minds, impresses itself upon their hearts and settles there, and reveals its effectiveness in the fulfillment of what it promises."[45] By the power of the Spirit, effective preaching changes the hearts of the hearers, and the change of heart is revealed in their altered behavior.

Moreover, not only the words of the worship leader, but also the words of the community are crucial elements in sacramental practice. Calvin insisted that an "outward confession" of faith should be part of the Lord's Supper. He interpreted Jesus' words "Do this in remembrance of me" to mean that we should "with a single voice . . . confess openly before men that for us the whole assurance of life and salvation rests upon the Lord's death, that we may glorify him by our confession. . . ."[46] It is important, in other words, that public corporate confession of faith be a part of the eucharistic liturgy in order to make

43. *Institutes* 4.14.4.

44. *Institutes* 4.17.15.

45. *Institutes* 4.17.39. For more on Calvin's insistence on edifying worship, see McKee, "Reformed Worship in the Sixteenth Century," p. 9.

46. *Institutes* 4.17.37.

clear the purpose of the sacrament. The words of the liturgy are indispensable in evoking the right attitude of the worshipers.

Words and symbols, or Word and sacrament, are the two principles that make up right worship, according to Calvin. This is quite clear from his discussions of eucharist. But it is equally clear that Word and sacrament cannot be effective unless they engage the worshiper. Word and sacrament do not operate in a void; they are intended to do something to the congregation. They are intended to convert people, to "beget faith."

Faith

This brings us to the last necessary element in Calvin's understanding of how the eucharist works: the receptivity of the worshiper, or faith.[47] This is indispensable, because without it, words and actions are in vain. If the preaching does not beget faith, then the person cannot partake of the sacrament worthily. He says in his "Short Treatise on the Lord's Supper," "Our souls ought to be oppressed by famine and to have desire and ardent longing to be fed, in order to find their proper nourishment in the Supper of the Lord."[48] If that desire and ardent longing are not present, then the soul cannot be nourished — and the ritual is ineffective. So also in the *Institutes* he says, "I deny that it [the Lord's Supper] can be eaten without some taste of faith."[49] The emphasis on faith is also clear in Calvin's order of the eucharist in the *Institutes*, in which the actions of eating and drinking are preceded by a prayer that "the Lord . . . teach and form us to receive [the Supper] with faith," and followed by an exhortation to faith and confession of faith.[50] All of these demonstrate that even when symbols and words are in perfect order, the eucharistic ritual requires faith in order to work.[51]

47. For a helpful discussion of Calvin on faith, see Gerrish, *Grace and Gratitude*, pp. 62-76.

48. "Short Treatise on the Lord's Supper," p. 151. For this same theme, see also Commentary on Ezekiel 20:20, in *Commentaries*, p. 233.

49. *Institutes* 4.17.33; cf. 4.17.40.

50. *Institutes* 4.17.43.

51. See Gerrish, *Grace and Gratitude*, pp. 138f. A recent work by Todd Murken de-

When considering the role of faith in Calvin's theology, it is critical to remember that Calvin does not understand faith to be a purely subjective individual state, but a gift of the Holy Spirit. His basic definition of faith makes this clear: faith is "a firm and certain knowledge of God's benevolence toward us, founded upon the truth of the freely given promise in Christ, both revealed to our minds and sealed upon our hearts through the Holy Spirit."[52] We do not achieve faith on our own, but only receive it. In this sense, faith is not simply subjective, but also objectively given. The gift of faith then enables us to receive the benefits of Christ. Faith is both the posture of receptivity by which we receive Christ and is itself a gift received.

At times, Calvin's emphasis on faith seems to detract from outward, corporate practice. Eucharistic practice becomes secondary to, or worse, an unnecessary appendage to, faith. For instance, in his discussion of the proper celebration of the Lord's Supper in the *Institutes,* Calvin says that the details of the actions are unimportant: "As for the outward ceremony of the action — whether or not the believers take it in their hands, or divide it among themselves, or severally eat what has been given to each; whether they hand the cup back to the deacon or give it to the next person; whether the bread is leavened or unleavened; the wine red or white — it makes no difference."[53] What is really important, claims Calvin, is the faith with which the sacrament is received. Here he suggests that the outward actions have little or no significance as long as the worshipers have faith. The focus here is on the internal receptivity of the individual worshiper rather than the worshiping community's actions. Therefore, as Kilian McDonnell points out in his study of Calvin's eucharistic theology, "Eucharistic eating becomes only a moment in that perpetual eating which takes place in faith."[54] There is no specific gift in the eucharist; what is received

---

velops in detail the understanding of faith in the Lord's Supper as "active receptivity," based primarily on Luther's writings but engaging a wide range of ecumenical eucharistic theology. See Todd B. Murken, *Take and Eat, and Take the Consequences: How Receiving the Lord's Supper Is an Action That Makes a Difference* (New York: Peter Lang, 2002).

52. *Institutes* 3.2.7.

53. *Institutes* 3.2.7.

54. McDonnell, *John Calvin, the Church, and the Eucharist,* p. 378. For a more sympathetic discussion of this same theme, see Wallace, *Calvin's Doctrine,* pp. 238f.

there is already received elsewhere by faith.[55] This theme in Calvin is certainly part of the reason that Reformed theologians have often de-emphasized rituals or sacraments: these are simply not seen as necessary, given the importance of faith. Such a focus does not encourage careful attention to the ritual dimension of the eucharist.

Related to this emphasis on individual faith is Calvin's focus on self-examination. Calvin is very concerned that worshipers partake of the eucharist worthily, and so he exhorts the congregation in his eucharistic liturgy:

> . . . let every man examine and prove his own conscience to see whether he truly repents of his faults and grieves over his sins, desiring to live henceforth a holy life according to God. Above all, let him see whether he has his trust in the mercy of God and seeks his salvation wholly in Jesus Christ and, renouncing all hatred and rancor, has high resolve and courage to live in peace and brotherly love with his neighbors.[56]

This exhortation precedes the distribution of the elements and is a distinctive mark of Reformed worship in the sixteenth century.[57] Like the emphasis on faith, this focus on individual self-examination seems to work against a focus on the eucharistic ritual itself. It can lead to a preoccupation with the status of the individual soul to the exclusion of the bodily actions of the worshiper. Calvin mentions this liturgical emphasis also in his "Short Treatise on the Lord's Supper": he notes that the right use of the sacrament "consists in observing the institution of our Lord with reverence," which means that all participants must examine themselves to determine their worthiness to partake.[58] Calvin goes on to remind his readers that no one can be truly worthy,

---

55. However, to claim that the eucharist does not impart a specific gift does not mean it is empty; if it is the focal instance of what we always receive from God, then that can be an argument for its necessity. It focuses our attention on what is always already there, but which we do not always perceive. (Stan Hall, private communication, May 2000.)

56. "Form of Church Prayers," p. 206.

57. This liturgical element appears in Presbyterian liturgies at least as recently as the 1921 *Book of Common Order* of the Presbyterian Church in the United States.

58. "Short Treatise on the Lord's Supper," p. 148.

so that it is sufficient to hope for salvation in Jesus Christ and to desire to live by the gospel, but the focus remains on the individual's interior state rather than the actions of the corporate body.[59]

But to read Calvin as a pious individualist, concerned only about the state of each person's soul and without regard for the practices of the community, is to distort his understanding of faith. As Elsie Anne McKee points out, Calvin's concern about worthy reception is not solely focused on the individual; rather, "Calvin insisted that what makes one fit to receive is not perfection but trust in Christ alone, along with repentance, and reconciliation with God and one's neighbors. . . . [T]he Supper is the meal of the whole body, not just those who happen to feel worthy on a given day, and therefore worthiness has a corporate dimension."[60] Faith is necessary for worthy reception, but such faith is not simply an isolated individualistic state.

We must remember that Calvin's concern for faith was a response to a situation in which he perceived too much emphasis being placed on the external details of the eucharist, without any attention to the role of the worshiper. His call for faith was a reminder that the eucharist does not work *ex opere operato,* as some external force independent of the people. In this respect he stands closer to Zwingli, who insisted that true sacramental eating is by faith, not by mouth. Unlike Zwingli, however, Calvin is clearly seeking a balance: of Word and sacrament, and of objective gift and subjective response.[61]

59. "Short Treatise on the Lord's Supper," p. 152. This critique is tempered somewhat by Bard Thompson's observation that in his eucharistic liturgy, Calvin was envisioning a gathering of "holy, elect people of God" rather than a "random gathering of Christians" (*Liturgies of the Western Church,* p. 193). Seen in this light, we begin to understand that even Calvin's apparent focus on interiority and the individual presupposed a particular corporate ritual context. Even so, Brooks Holifield notes that this emphasis of Calvin's did lay the groundwork for "a markedly introspective sacramental piety" that became characteristic of Reformed eucharistic devotion. See E. Brooks Holifield, *The Covenant Sealed: The Development of Puritan Sacramental Theology in Old and New England, 1520-1720* (New Haven and London: Yale University Press, 1974), p. 19. This sort of introspective piety persists today in the understanding of the Lord's Supper as individual devotion, described in chapter four.

60. McKee, "Reformed Worship in the Sixteenth Century," p. 22. See also her discussion on pp. 29-30.

61. Zwingli himself came to a fuller appreciation for the work of God in the eucharist at the end of his life, according to one biographer. In his posthumously published

Faith is not itself union with Christ; it is the "longing," the "taste" for communion with the divine. It is the attitude of receptivity, given by the Holy Spirit, which allows the Word and sacrament to join the person to Christ. Note, too, that the exhortation to self-examination in Calvin's eucharistic liturgy is not ultimately focused on the interior of the soul; it is oriented toward life in community: "Above all, let [each person] see whether he has his trust in the mercy of God and seeks his salvation wholly in Jesus Christ and, renouncing all hatred and rancor, has high resolve and courage *to live in peace and brotherly love with his neighbors.*"[62] Faith is not opposed to corporate practice. It is a necessary component of that practice.

Relationship with God

Calvin, like all the reformers, proposed changes in the liturgy precisely because he understood it to be of crucial importance in establishing right relationship between the worshipers and God. When worship — or, we might say, when the central Christian ritual — is not done "decently and in order," the relationship between the people and God is jeopardized. This is what had happened in the Roman Catholic mass, according to Calvin. As Jasper and Cuming point out in their edition of *Prayers of the Eucharist,* the texts of the Roman rite underwent no significant change from the eighth to the sixteenth century, but

in the West the way in which that Roman text was used and the meanings which gathered around it changed considerably. For example, the active participation of the laity virtually disappeared, the eucharist becoming a spectacle, overlaid with cere-

---

Exposition of the Faith (1536), he said, "By this commemoration all the benefits which God has displayed in his Son are called to mind. And by the signs themselves, the bread and wine, Christ himself is as it were set before our eyes, so that not merely with the ear, but with eye and palate we see and taste that Christ whom the soul bears within itself and in whom it rejoices" (George, *Theology of the Reformers,* p. 157, quoting H. Wayne Pipkin, "The Positive Religious Values of Zwingli's Eucharistic Writings," in E. J. Furcha, ed., *Huldrych Zwingli, 1484-1531: A Legacy of Radical Reform* [Montreal: McGill University Faculty of Religious Studies, 1985], p. 127).

62. "The Form of Church Prayers," p. 206.

monies and symbolism unknown to the early church: communion itself becoming a rare occurrence, being supplanted by the elevation and adoration of the consecrated elements: and the Mass was regarded as a sacrifice in itself, additional to that offered by Jesus Christ on Calvary.[63]

Though this may oversimplify the official interpretation of the Roman mass, it certainly describes what the reformers saw in the late medieval period. Calvin objected to all of these changes, yearning for a return to the simplicity and power of the early church's liturgy. He contended that the right performance of the liturgy was of critical importance in uniting the faithful community with God.

Calvin states as much in his explanation of the purposes of the Lord's Supper. In the "Short Treatise," he lists three purposes of the eucharist: 1) spiritual nourishment, in which we are united with Christ, 2) incitement to gratitude for all God's goodness to us, and 3) exhortation to holy living and to mutual love.[64] In other words, we celebrate the Lord's Supper in the conviction that through this meal, the Holy Spirit establishes right relationship among persons and between persons and God. Calvin understood the eucharist as a necessarily corporate act, so that it strengthens the community itself in addition to nourishing the bonds between the community and God.

At many other points, Calvin lifts up union with God in Christ as the point of the eucharist. For instance, as cited above, he asks "What is the purpose of . . . the whole external order of the church except to unite us with God?"[65] And elsewhere, "The analogy of the sign applies only if souls find their nourishment in Christ — which cannot happen unless Christ truly grows into one with us, and refreshes us by the eating of his flesh and the drinking of his blood."[66] As these passages show, the

---

63. R. C. D. Jasper and G. J. Cuming, eds., *Prayers of the Eucharist: Early and Reformed*, 3rd ed. (Collegeville, Minn.: The Liturgical Press, 1990), p. 177.

64. "Short Treatise on the Lord's Supper," p. 144. Cf. Wallace, *Calvin's Doctrine*, pp. 240f., where he lists the following three aspects of the sacraments' usefulness: 1) "they assist spiritual growth by uniting us more fully to Christ the more they are used by faith," 2) "they confirm and increase the faith of believers," and 3) "they are a spur to practical Christian living," especially as an incentive to unity of love.

65. Commentary on Psalm 24:7-8, in *Commentaries*, p. 393.

66. *Institutes* 4.17.10.

eucharist in Calvin's estimation does not just remind us of something or re-enact a previously stated doctrine. By the power of the Spirit, it accomplishes something: union with Christ and with one another.

But who is this God with whom we are united in the eucharist, the God in whom we are to have faith? Here is a final area in which Calvin achieves a remarkable balance, for God is simultaneously free *from* and free *for* involvement with creation. Calvin proclaims that God is free, omnipotent, lord of all things. Everything that is owes its existence to God, who alone rules over creation:

> . . . not only does he sustain this universe (as he once founded it) by his boundless might, regulate it by his wisdom, preserve it by his goodness, and especially rule mankind by his righteousness and judgment, bear with it in his mercy, watch over it by his protection; but also . . . no drop will be found either of wisdom and light, or of righteousness or power or rectitude, or of genuine truth, which does not flow from him, and of which he is not the cause.[67]

Because God alone both generates and cares for creation, nothing humans do can limit God's love or constrain God's actions.

Precisely because of such divine sovereignty, God (in Christ by the Spirit) unites with humanity in the eucharist, according to Calvin. Not subject to natural laws or human reason, God is able to be spiritually present in the sacrament. One of Calvin's Lutheran opponents, Joachim Westphal, had accused him of having a eucharistic theology dictated by reason, since he will not admit of a literal identification of the bread with Christ's body. In response, Calvin protests:

> We say Christ descends to us both by the outward symbol and by his Spirit, that he may truly quicken our souls by the substance of his flesh and of his blood . . . nothing is more beyond the natural than that souls should borrow spiritual and heavenly life from a flesh that had its origin from earth, and underwent death. There is nothing more incredible than that things severed and removed from one another by the whole space between heaven and earth

67. *Institutes* 1.2.1.

should not only be connected across such a great distance but also be united, so that souls may receive nourishment from Christ's flesh. Therefore, let perverse men cease to engender hatred toward us by the foul misstatement that with wicked intent we would somewhat restrict God's boundless power.[68]

The sovereign power of the Holy Spirit is precisely what unites us with Christ in the eucharist. Far from limiting divine power, says Calvin, he is proclaiming the "boundless power" of God.

Ironically, whereas Calvin's contemporary critics accused him of limiting God's sovereignty in his eucharistic doctrine, a twentieth-century critic accused him of maintaining so much divine sovereignty that he eliminates any real sacramental presence in the eucharist. According to Kilian McDonnell, Calvin's devotion to God's sovereignty prevents him from understanding Christ to be really present in the sacrament: "The evangelical passion for God's freedom and sovereignty made it impossible for Calvin to conceive of God committing himself to a sacramental engagement of real incarnational dimensions. God is not bound; what is more, God cannot bind himself! Calvin will not permit it."[69] Ronald Wallace agrees, though in more moderate language, saying that Calvin wants to avoid any suggestion that the grace of God could be bound up with or included in the sacraments, "that here careless human initiative could cause divine action, or mechanical operation could produce divine grace."[70] This reading of Calvin focuses on his caution about idolatry of the sacrament; he denied the literal physical presence of Christ in the eucharist because he wanted people to worship God, not bread. Therefore he emphasized that "God is not bound," that God is supremely free of all necessary connection to the sacramental elements.

However, it does not follow, as McDonnell claims, that "God cannot bind himself" in Calvin's theology. Just because there is no necessary connection between God and the material elements does not mean that Christ is not present in the eucharist. Rather, as Calvin himself said, in the eucharist, "Christ descends to us both by the out-

68. *Institutes* 4.17.24.
69. McDonnell, *John Calvin, the Church, and the Eucharist*, p. 370.
70. Wallace, *Calvin's Doctrine*, p. 164. See also Holifield, *The Covenant Sealed*, p. 18.

ward symbol and by his Spirit, that he may truly quicken our souls by the substance of his flesh and of his blood."[71] God — in Christ through the Holy Spirit — is present in the sacrament precisely because of divine freedom. God is not only free *from* involvement with creation, but free *for* such material involvement.[72]

This focus on divine sovereignty forces us to take a new look at the material elements and actions of the eucharist because they may be mediators of the divine presence — not in and of themselves, but by the action of the Spirit. Calvin was addressing the idolatry of the material elements of the eucharist, and in particular, the consecrated host. Therefore he denied that God could be bound by material elements. But he did not deny God's presence in the sacrament. Our context is different and our idolatry different: whereas sixteenth-century Roman Catholic practice led people to worship the host, according to Calvin, late twentieth- and early twenty-first-century Protestant practice too often leads people to worship their own reason.[73] We tend to focus on proper understanding of the eucharist, implying that right understanding is what makes the sacrament effective. Our idolatry of reason has led us to think that the eucharist is *our* action, but Calvin maintains that it is God's. If this sacrament is understood as God's, if God really works in the sacrament, then it is important to attend to the physical and verbal details of the sacrament to discern what God may be doing. And this is precisely what constitutes a ritual reading of the eucharist. Rather than focusing solely on the proper doctrinal formulations to prepare congregants for the eucharist, we need to focus also on the objects and actions through which the Spirit may work to unite the people with Christ.[74]

71. *Institutes* 4.17.24.

72. This interpretation is consistent with Barth's discussion of divine freedom in *Church Dogmatics* II.1: *The Doctrine of God* (Edinburgh: T. & T. Clark, 1957), paragraph 28. Christopher Elwood makes a similar point in a very different context when he says, "We must remember that the God portrayed in Calvin's writings, although free from containment within the created world, is nonetheless intimately involved in the temporal causal nexus" (*The Body Broken: The Calvinist Doctrine of the Eucharist and the Symbolization of Power in Sixteenth-Century France* [New York: Oxford University Press, 1999],p. 75).

73. To be sure, idolatry of reason is not the only idolatry that needs criticism in our context. North American Protestants are also remarkably prone to idolatry of feeling and individual experience. But this is not the focus of the current project.

74. Late medieval nominalists such as William of Ockham made a similar connection between God's sovereignty and the need for empirical observation. "If God can

Calvin's pneumatology is particularly relevant to a consideration of the God with whom we are united in the eucharist.[75] This is closely related to the theme of God's sovereignty; divine sovereignty allows God to transcend natural boundaries to be present in the eucharist, and the Holy Spirit is the specific way in which God is present, according to Calvin. The Holy Spirit is God's power and presence in the community of faith, particularly though not solely in the sacraments. As he says in his commentary on Ephesians, "We are not bone of [Christ's] bone, and flesh of His flesh, because, like ourselves, He is man, but because, by the power of His Spirit, He engrafts us into His body, so that from him we derive life."[76] It is not the mere fact of Christ's humanity that makes us one with him, but the action of the Holy Spirit which unites us with him. With regard to the eucharist in particular, Calvin explains in the *Institutes* that we participate in Christ's body through the power of the Holy Spirit, which can unite things separated by space.[77] While Christ is not locally present in the elements, we participate in Christ's body in the eucharist through the Spirit, which is "like a channel through which all that Christ himself is and has is conveyed to us."[78] McDonnell points out that the Spirit op-

---

do anything *de potentia sua absoluta,* then we have to observe to see what in fact God has done *de potentia sua ordinata.*" The fact that God is not constrained by our reason or natural laws means that we must look carefully to see what in fact God is doing in the world. I am indebted to Dr. Walter L. Moore, Jr., for this observation. For a brief discussion of the distinction between *potentia ordinata* and *potentia absoluta,* see Steven Ozment, *The Age of Reform 1250-1550: An Intellectual and Religious History of Late Medieval and Reformation Europe* (New Haven: Yale University Press, 1980), pp. 38ff.

75. See Gerrish, *Grace and Gratitude,* pp. 137f. James White notes that although Calvin makes the Spirit central to his eucharistic theology, it is not central to the liturgy itself (*Sacraments as God's Self-Giving* [Nashville: Abingdon, 1983], p. 60). It is telling that for the local congregation I studied, the reverse is true: although the Spirit makes a prominent appearance in the liturgy, it is virtually absent from the articulated theology of the congregation. Be that as it may, Calvin's strong pneumatology can still provide a resource for refocusing on the ritual dimension of the eucharist, which may affect liturgical practices in our day. This is a good example of how secondary theology can have a positive effect on primary theology.

76. Commentary on Ephesians 5:28-33, in *The Epistles of Paul to the Galatians, Ephesians, Philippians, and Colossians,* trans. T. H. L. Parker, ed. David W. Torrance and Thomas F. Torrance, Calvin's Commentaries (Edinburgh: Oliver & Boyd, 1965), p. 209.

77. *Institutes* 4.17.10.

78. *Institutes* 4.17.12.

erates in two ways in the eucharist: it makes the believers worthy and it makes Christ's body present.[79] By sanctifying the believers and making present the substance of Christ's body, the Holy Spirit brings together things that are separated by space.

The use of the plural "we" and "us" in the preceding passages is no accident. Calvin placed the emphasis on the role of the Holy Spirit in the community of faith, not just in the hearts of individual believers. Calvin had a profound appreciation for the corporate nature of the church. This was another reason for his rejection of the simple identification of Christ's body with the eucharistic bread: he was more interested in identifying Christ's body through the Spirit's power with the corporate body of the church. Thus, although McDonnell criticizes Calvin for maintaining too much distance between "sign" (bread) and "signified" (Christ),[80] it may be that this distance allows us to notice the presence of the Holy Spirit in the broader community rather than in the material elements alone. As Alasdair Heron points out, for Calvin the real meaning of the eucharist is not the "connexion between the body of Christ and the bread" but "the whole relation between Christ and us."[81] Calvin's eucharistic interest was social rather than metaphysical.

This emphasis on the role of the Holy Spirit in the community is a helpful resource for recovering the ritual dimension of the eucharist because, as with God's sovereignty, the work of the Spirit calls attention to the objectivity of the eucharistic event. A focus on the Spirit shifts our perspective so that, instead of the sacrament being a purely human activity governed by an overriding concern for proper understanding, it becomes a transforming event in a community powerfully charged with the divine presence. And once we recover some objectivity in the eucharist, we begin to notice the meanings, gestures, micro-events that arise in the moment of celebration which may or may not be connected to the official explanation of what is going on. We begin to realize that something is happening here that is not entirely within our control. This is to move toward a ritual reading of the eucharist.

79. McDonnell, *John Calvin, the Church, and the Eucharist,* p. 364.

80. McDonnell, *John Calvin, the Church, and the Eucharist,* p. 368.

81. Alasdair I. C. Heron, *Table and Tradition: Toward an Ecumenical Understanding of the Eucharist* (Philadelphia: Westminster Press, 1983), p. 127.

Calvin: Some Conclusions

The Lord's Supper, according to Calvin, is a primary event shaping people into communities oriented to God. In the Supper, by the power of the Spirit and through the spoken and embodied Word, Christ comes to the assembled people, and those who have a "taste of faith" receive him and are changed. Ideally, the Word proclaimed by the preacher will draw the congregation's attention to the gift of Christ and move them to receive that gift more fully and respond in gratitude. The sacrament, with its gestures of giving and receiving nourishment, cultivates in the congregation the embodied knowledge that all of life is gift, is grace. Such knowledge of life as gift and God as the gracious donor is itself faith, and this faith is renewed at each eucharistic celebration. But none of this happens automatically; it is only through the work of the Holy Spirit that faith is formed and renewed. It is only through the mysterious presence of God that any communication between human and divine transpires at all.

This is the theology articulated by Calvin, intended to reflect the true nature of eucharistic worship and to help people become more ardent participants in the eucharist. How does it relate to the ordinary everyday communion service described in the prologue? A fuller discussion of that liturgy will form the substance of chapter four, but with regard to Calvin's own eucharistic theology, a few observations are appropriate here. To begin with, Word and sacrament are fairly balanced and integrated; the proclaimed Word points toward sacramental participation, and the sacrament is offered in such a way that attentive worshipers cannot miss the crucial gestures of taking, blessing, breaking, and giving. As Calvin would wish, audible words and visible and tangible symbols conspire to move participants toward fuller appreciation of the gifts of God. There are hints, however, that Word (written and proclaimed) and sacrament (construed as symbolic object and action) are not valued equally in this setting. In the prologue, both ministers take great care in preparing the words of the liturgy, whether or not they write them all down. It is clear that both are concerned that what they say is clearly heard and understood by the congregational members. The words are direct and forceful. By contrast, the sacramental elements are minimal: a small roll to break, a little juice to pour from pitcher to chalice, tiny squares of bread that bear little resemblance to the symbolic loaf broken by the pastor. Furthermore, although the gestures of blessing and breaking the bread convey appropriate generosity, the handling of bread and juice by elders and people displays more than a little anxiety. Elders are anxious about distributing the elements in the proper manner and as efficiently as possible, while some of the people in the pew are unsure how to pass the trays and whether or not to sing in the process. Little attention has been given to enabling the congregation's fully embodied and intentional participation. All of this suggests that the Word is more important than the sacrament. Words are large, carefully chosen, direct; visible and tangible symbols are small, carefully controlled, and anxiety-making. Given this imbalance in the treatment of Word and sacrament, the observer wonders how (and whether!) sacramental participation is forming people in faith.

These observations about the relative status of Word and sacrament in this congregation's practice are, of course, broad generalizations that require a great deal more nuance. Also, while eucharistic performance, including the relationship of Word and sacrament, can be observed, the relationship between such performance and faith is much more difficult to detect. Further exploration of this area will follow in chapter four. Suffice it to say at this time, however, that Calvin's principle of the balance of Word and sacrament raises questions about the practice of communion in this church. At the same time, his insistence that God does work in and through material objects and actions to form faith stands as an important reminder that God can work not only with our best ritual efforts, but also in spite of them. With appropriate humility, then, we must attend to what is going on in actual communities of faith like this one, in order that we may discern how their eucharistic practices are shaping people in their relationships to God and one another.

Throughout his eucharistic theology, Calvin struggles to emphasize both Word and sacrament, both faith and practice, and both divine transcendence and divine incarnation. While he does at points emphasize doctrine as prior to practice, or Word as the "substance" of sacrament, these must be understood as polemical outbursts in the context of his particular situation. Our situation is different, and rather than appropriating his polemical tone against a medieval mass that no longer exists, we would do well rather to strive for his attention to both Word and sacrament. In our time, as increasing numbers of Reformed Christians are coming to discern, a situation that needs redressing is an over-emphasis on doctrine and a neglect of respect for practice as a place where God chooses to work. While Calvin insisted that God works through both *Word* and sacrament, we need reminding that God works through both Word and *sacrament.*

Later Developments in the Reformed Tradition

Some of Calvin's successors seem to have focused on right doctrine without the same balance that Calvin tried to achieve. Faith became closely identified with adherence to correct doctrine, and eucharistic practice gradually became secondary to proper understanding. This tendency can be seen, for instance, in the works of Francis Turretin and Charles Hodge. Other Reformed theologians, however, strove to uphold Calvin's attention to the centrality of eucharistic practice; most prominent among this latter group is the Mercersburg theologian John Williamson Nevin. A quick overview of these three figures in Reformed history will demonstrate how Calvin's eucharistic theology was interpreted by later generations.

Francis Turretin and Protestant Scholasticism

Francis Turretin (1623-1687) represents the epitome of seventeenth-century Protestant scholasticism, with its concern for precision in doctrine and its use of a theological method greatly influenced by Thomas Aquinas. Turretin, the son of a Swiss pastor and theologian, became himself a pastor and later professor of theology in Geneva. During his life, the church in Geneva felt threatened both externally, by France and its Catholic king, and internally, by Reformed theologians who were inclined to compromise on distinctive Reformed points of doctrine. In this climate, Turretin emerged as "the brightest and most articulate defender of the traditional Reformed vision."[82]

82. Timothy R. Phillips, "The Dissolution of Francis Turretin's Vision of *Theologia*: Geneva at the End of the Seventeenth Century," in *The Identity of Geneva: The Christian*

He was seen both in his own day and by later generations as a defender of high Calvinist orthodoxy. In the nineteenth century, Archibald Alexander and Charles Hodge at Princeton and Robert Dabney at Union Theological Seminary in Virginia used his massive *Institutes of Elenctic Theology* as their basic theology textbook, influencing generations of American Presbyterian pastors in their understanding of the Reformed tradition. Turretin was, by his own admission, a polemical theologian, engaged in articulating the true faith against a range of possible distortions, including "Romanism," Lutheranism, Socinianism, and rationalism. The very term "elenctic" was taken from the Greek *elenxis,* "conviction, rebuke, or reproof," so elenctic theology was directly concerned with "refutation of errors."[83]

Although Turretin in his *Institutes* refuted errors of doctrine on both the Roman Catholic and Socinian sides, in his sections on the church and sacraments, almost all of his polemics are against the "Romanists" and their close alignment of church and sacraments with the presence of God. So much of his effort was devoted to distinguishing God from the visible church and the visible signs in the sacraments that he neglected Calvin's attention to the opposite problem: too little regard for the signs. In Turretin's theology, word precedes sacrament, faith and doctrine precede practice, and God works through the mind, to faith, in a spiritual manner that does not require material objects and actions.

While Calvin did at times claim that word was prior to sacrament, establishing it and constituting its "substance," Turretin consistently asserted this side of Calvin's theology. To the question "Was it necessary that sacraments should be instituted in the church and is their use necessary?" Turretin responded that the word itself needed no confirmation, but God wished to seal the certainty of grace by all our senses, not just by hearing. The sacraments are "to help our infirmity and con-

---

Commonwealth 1564-1864, ed. John B. Roney and Martin I. Klauber (Westport, Conn.: Greenwood Press, 1998), p. 77.

83. See James T. Dennison, Jr., "The Life and Career of Francis Turretin," in Francis Turretin, *Institutes of Elenctic Theology,* vol. 3, trans. George Musgrave Giger, ed. James T. Dennison, Jr. (Phillipsburg, N.J.: Presbyterian and Reformed Publishing Company, 1997), p. 647. For the Greek, see William F. Arndt and F. Wilbur Gingrich, *A Greek-English Lexicon of the New Testament and Other Early Christian Literature,* 2nd ed. (Chicago: University of Chicago Press, 1957, 1979), p. 249.

firm our faith."[84] In this argument he echoed Calvin's own assertion that we have sacraments because of our weakness, just as we have words because of our ignorance.[85] So our human nature does require both words and sacraments. But Turretin subtly changed Calvin's theology in two ways here. First, he did not treat word and sacrament equally as addressed to our human nature, but called the word "divine and infallible" while the sacraments are merely accommodations to our infirmity. Word seems to stand above reproof, while sacraments are grudgingly admitted to be necessary because of our human failings. Second, he specified that sacraments do not produce faith, but confirm it. They are strictly secondary to the operation of the word. So, although Turretin initially acknowledged the human need for sacraments, he quickly went on to clarify that sacraments are subordinated to the word. In this he disrupted the balance that Calvin usually sought between word and sacrament, the sacrament as word made visible and the word as "written . . . with the blood of the Son of God."[86]

Turretin also altered Calvin's depiction of faith and its relation to liturgical practices. While Calvin tended to describe faith as the Spirit-given attitude of receptivity to the working of God, Turretin tended to link faith to knowledge of doctrine, which in his view always precedes the practices of the church. "Now although the knowledge of the church is especially necessary to us, still it must not be supposed that it ought to precede the examination and knowledge of doctrine, so that *faith or doctrine* ought to be known from the church rather than the church from the *doctrine and faith*."[87] Doctrine and faith are the critical principles that allow one to know the church. They come first, and knowledge of the church comes afterward. A bit later, Turretin continued:

84. *Institutes of Elenctic Theology*, vol. 3, Topic 19, question 2, p. 343. It is important to note that "word" in this translation is uncapitalized, and in this context does not seem to refer to Christ the Word, but to scripture, both written and read. So when Turretin describes the word as divine and infallible here, he is not referring to Christ, but to scripture.

85. See above, note 32.

86. See above, note 29.

87. *Institutes of Elenctic Theology*, vol. 3, p. 3. In the same section he states clearly, "The unity of the church supposes a preceding unity of faith in which believers are joined."

> It is one thing to know the church with a confused knowledge as an assembly of men professing the same doctrine and using the same sacred rites; another to know the same by a distinct knowledge as an assembly of believers retaining the true *faith and doctrine* of Christ. In the former sense, we confess the knowledge of the church precedes the knowledge of faith; but in the latter, we deny it because the truth of the church rests upon the truth of faith.[88]

Public practices, profession of faith and "sacred rites," do not constitute the church. Maintenance of true faith and doctrine constitute the church. Turretin was concerned here primarily with the claims of the Roman Catholic Church to be the one true church, through which faith and doctrine were mediated. To counter this, Turretin argued strongly for the priority of "faith and doctrine," a critical principle that allows for the church to be judged. Important though this was, Turretin's insistence on the priority of faith and doctrine to the church and its practices led to two problematic tendencies that continue to haunt Reformed Protestantism today: the close identification of faith with assent to propositional statements and the relegation of external practices to secondary status, as the expression of prior belief.[89]

Finally, Turretin spiritualized Calvin's depiction of the union of believers and Christ in the eucharist. Though he did describe communion as nourishing the union of believers with Christ,[90] Turretin emphasized that the union has nothing to do with the physical, but is through the mind, to faith, in a manner only tenuously connected with the signs. Sacraments are "sacred visible signs and seals divinely instituted to signify and seal to our consciences the promises of saving grace in Christ and in turn to testify to our faith and piety and obedience towards God."[91] As for Calvin, sacraments in Turretin's view consisted of sign and signified, the "sign" being the material symbols of bread and wine, and the "signified" being Christ himself. But Turretin was even more

88. *Institutes of Elenctic Theology,* vol. 3, p. 5. Emphases mine.

89. For the classic critique of faith as assent to propositional statements, see George Lindbeck, *The Nature of Doctrine: Religion and Theology in a Postliberal Age* (Philadelphia: Westminster Press, 1984), esp. chapter 5.

90. *Institutes of Elenctic Theology,* vol. 3, p. 429.

91. *Institutes of Elenctic Theology,* vol. 3, p. 339.

concerned than Calvin to distinguish these two. Signs differ from signified in nature and properties, in object, and in mode of communication.[92] The relationship between sign and signified is due to "signification, sealing, and exhibition." There is nothing in Turretin's language to parallel Calvin's emphasis on "engrafting," on communication of Christ's very substance to the believer through the power of the Holy Spirit. Indeed, Turretin says very little about the work of the Holy Spirit in connection with the "holy Supper" at all. God communicates with the mind, by way of analogy. Turretin gives the impression that if God works through the eucharist, it is to represent Christ to our minds, to strengthen our faith, but not to communicate Christ's flesh to ours.

Turretin the elenctic theologian illustrates the movement of Reformed sacramental theology away from Calvin's attempt at balance and toward a greater emphasis on Word over sacrament, doctrine as prior to practice, and sacramental union with Christ as having to do with mind and human spirit rather than material reality. His approach informed Reformed eucharistic theology for many generations, appearing perhaps most notably in the nineteenth-century theologian Charles Hodge.

John Williamson Nevin and Charles Hodge

In the mid-nineteenth century, a eucharistic debate erupted in American Reformed theology which illuminates the continuing struggle for balance so clear in Calvin's writings. In 1846, John Williamson Nevin, professor of theology at the German Reformed seminary in Mercersburg, Pennsylvania, published a book entitled *The Mystical Presence: A Vindication of the Reformed or Calvinistic Doctrine of the Holy Eucharist.*[93]

92. *Institutes of Elenctic Theology,* vol. 3, p. 340.

93. John Williamson Nevin, *The Mystical Presence: A Vindication of the Reformed or Calvinistic Doctrine of the Holy Eucharist* (originally published in Philadelphia: J. B. Lippincott & Co., 1846; reprinted in Eugene, Ore.: Wipf & Stock, 2000). Hereafter cited as *Mystical Presence.* For a lucid summary of Nevin's eucharistic theology, see Arie J. Griffioen, "Nevin on the Lord's Supper," in *Reformed Confessionalism in Nineteenth Century America,* ed. Sam Hamstra, Jr., and Arie J. Griffioen (Lanham, Md.: Scarecrow Press, 1995), pp. 113-24. For a recent biography of Nevin, see D. G. Hart, *John Williamson Nevin: High Church Calvinist* (Phillipsburg, N.J.: P. & R. Publishing, 2005).

In it he argued strongly for a recovery of appreciation for the work of Christ through the eucharist, and against what he perceived to be an "unchurchly, rationalistic tendency" that had invaded the church in his day.[94] Two years later, Charles Hodge, eminent professor of theology at Princeton, responded with a savage review of the book in the *Princeton Review*.[95] Hodge described Nevin's work as "an entire rejection not only of the peculiar doctrines of the Reformed church . . . but of some of the leading principles of Protestant, and even Catholic, theology in general."[96] It is significant that Hodge learned theology at Princeton from Archibald Alexander, who used Turretin's *Institutes* as a textbook, and Hodge himself used Turretin as the basic theology text in his classroom until the completion of his own *Systematic Theology* in 1872.[97] Nevin's argument and Hodge's critique of it provide a useful example of the tension within the Reformed tradition over the role of the eucharist. At the same time, Nevin stands as a significant theologian who tried to maintain Calvin's respect for the place of the eucharist against a competing American Reformed view that emphasized doctrine over practice.[98]

It is important to remember that Nevin and Hodge did agree on

94. *Mystical Presence*, p. 48.

95. Charles Hodge, review of *Mystical Presence* in *Princeton Review* 20 (April 1848): 227-78. For further reading on Hodge's theology, see the essays in *Charles Hodge Revisited: A Critical Appraisal of His Life and Work,* ed. John W. Stewart and James H. Moorhead (Grand Rapids: Eerdmans, 2002).

96. Hodge, review of *Mystical Presence*, p. 264.

97. See Dennison, "The Life and Career of Francis Turretin," p. 648.

98. Beginning in 1857, a similar contrast in sacramental views emerged in the South between John Adger at Columbia (Presbyterian) Seminary and Robert Dabney at Union Theological Seminary in Virginia. Adger taught his students a modified form of Nevin's doctrine of the mystical presence of Christ in the eucharist, while Dabney followed Turretin and Hodge in insisting that in the eucharist the Holy Spirit moves to elicit similar "graces, affections, and volitions" in the believer as in Christ, and that this similarity of spiritual life constitutes their unity. In a manner consistent with both Turretin and Hodge, Dabney defined the union of communicants with Christ "in such a way that eucharistic communion became little more than a didactic message designed to produce an inward comprehension of doctrinal truths with correspondingly appropriate emotional reactions." These two strands of the Reformed tradition shaped the theology and practice of a generation of Southern Presbyterian ministers in rather different ways. See E. Brooks Holifield, *The Gentlemen Theologians: American Theology in Southern Culture, 1795-1860* (Durham, N.C.: Duke University Press, 1978), p. 181; for an account of the contrast between Dabney and Adger, see pp. 175-83.

some things. Both were reacting against a common threat they perceived in American church life: the evangelical revivalism championed by Charles Finney. Both Nevin and Hodge judged that revivalism focused too much on the subjective dimension of the Christian life, without adequate attention to the objective work of God in Christ. In response, both emphasized the objectivity of Christ's work, which does not depend on us. Yet in spite of their common enemy, Nevin and Hodge came to disagree sharply in their understanding of the sacraments and the way the Spirit works through them to unite us with Christ.[99]

According to Nevin, the predominant view of the sacraments in American Protestantism of his time was as follows: "Baptism and the Lord's Supper are looked upon as mere outward signs, in the case of which all proper efficacy is supposed to be previously at hand in the inward state of the subject by whom they are received."[100] He called this view "Puritan" and "rationalistic," emphasizing the subjective state of the worshiper rather than the objective gift in the sacraments. He contrasted this view with the fuller sacramental theology of the sixteenth century, and especially of Calvin himself. This he stated early in his treatise: "The sacramental doctrine of the primitive Reformed Church stands inseparably connected with the idea of an inward living union between believers and Christ, in virtue of which they are incorporated into his very nature, and made to subsist with him by the power of a common life. In full correspondence with this conception of the Christian salvation . . . it was held that nothing less than such a real participation of [Christ's] living person is involved always in the right use of the Lord's Supper."[101] In the eucharist, the Holy Spirit communicates the life of Christ to believers, conforming them more and more closely to Christ's image. This does not depend on the subjective state of the believer, but on the working of God.

This claim made Hodge profoundly nervous. To claim such power for the eucharist was to wander into the land of "Romanists" and Lutherans, he warned. "Eating Christ's body and blood" simply means

---

99. See Peter J. Wallace, "History and Sacrament: John Williamson Nevin and Charles Hodge on the Lord's Supper," *Mid-America Journal of Theology* 11 (2000): 171-201.

100. *Mystical Presence,* p. 101.

101. *Mystical Presence,* pp. 50-51.

having faith in Christ, and so eating Christ occurs whenever one believes in Christ. There is no "special benefit or communion" to be had in the eucharist.[102] Such a position ascribes far too much power to the church and restricts the free working of God. "The main question whether we come to Christ, and then to the church; whether we by a personal act of faith receive him and by union with him become a member of his mystical body; or whether all our access to Christ is through a mediating church, Dr. Nevin decides against the evangelical system."[103] The proper evangelical view is that we come first to Christ and then to the church, not the other way around.[104]

"Well, yes," Nevin might say to Hodge at this point, "except that what you are describing as the 'evangelical system' is in fact a rationalistic corruption of the pure Reformed doctrine of the church and its sacraments. We cannot come to Christ apart from the church, because the church itself is the continuation of the life of Christ in the world." Or, to use Nevin's own words: "The life of the single Christian can be real and healthful only as it is born from the general life of the church. . . . An outward church is the necessary form of the new creation in Christ Jesus, in its very nature."[105] The church and its sacraments, by the power of the Spirit, convey the life of Christ to individual believers, not the other way around.

Nevin and Hodge did not argue explicitly over the relationship of Word and sacrament. While this balance was crucial to Calvin in the sixteenth century, it was not the central issue in the nineteenth-century context. We can see, however, a similar concern for balance of

---

102. Hodge, review of *Mystical Presence*, p. 247. In this position, Hodge was very close to Zwingli's and Oecolampadius' Marburg position, which questioned the usefulness of bodily eating when what was really necessary was spiritual eating, or faith. (See Sasse, *This Is My Body*, pp. 236, 239.) And Calvin himself at times seemed to deny any "special gift" in the eucharist, as Kilian McDonnell argues and as discussed above (see note 54). Hodge also, knowingly or unknowingly, presented here the "modern Puritan view" against which Nevin argued so forcefully: "in the modern Puritan view . . . this specific peculiar virtue of the sacraments is not recognized. . . . The idea of a peculiar sacramental power, belonging to this form of worship as such, seems to have no place at all in [this] system" (*Mystical Presence*, p. 112).

103. Hodge, review of *Mystical Presence*, p. 273.

104. In this assertion, Hodge is clearly influenced by Turretin's argument in his *Institutes of Elenctic Theology*, vol. 3, pp. 1-3, discussed above.

105. *Mystical Presence*, pp. 4, 5.

Word and sacrament in Nevin's consistent call for respect for objective sacramental power in a time when so much focus was placed on subjective understanding. For instance, he contrasted the "old Reformed view," which respected the mysterious work of the Spirit in the eucharist, with the "proper Puritan standpoint," which emphasized intelligibility of the sacrament. To demonstrate his point, he quoted Timothy Dwight as an exponent of the Puritan view:

> [The ends proposed in the Supper are] the enlargement, and rectification, of our *views,* — the purification of our *affections,* — the amendment of our *lives.* The means are efficacious and desirable; at the same time, simple; *intelligible to the humblest capacity;* in no respect burdensome; lying within the reach of all men; incapable of being misconstrued without violence; and therefore, not easily susceptible of *mystical* or superstitious perversion. In their own proper, undisguised nature, they appeal powerfully to the *senses,* the *imagination,* and the *heart;* and at the same time, enlighten, in the happiest manner, the *understanding.*[106]

Clearly, Nevin regarded such emphasis on the intelligibility of the sacrament as misguided; it draws the attention to human understanding rather than God's mysterious power through the event itself.

It is also clear from Nevin's derisive use of this passage that he was concerned to preserve the unity of human nature, body and soul. Like Calvin, Nevin described the purpose of the eucharist as union of believers with Christ, and this union involves more than rational understanding; it involves the whole person. So not only does a balance of Word and sacrament help to focus on divine as well as human activity, but it also emphasizes the engagement of the whole person, body as well as mind. This concern surfaces again later in *The Mystical Presence* when Nevin contrasts "life" and "doctrine": "This want of proportion between *life* and *doctrine,* is itself a great evil; especially now when the strong tide of rationalistic error, arrogating to itself the title of Protestant orthodoxy, is threatening to rarefy and spiritualize the whole truth into a sheer moral abstraction."[107] Nevin wanted to avoid

---

106. Dwight, quoted in *Mystical Presence,* p. 113. Emphases Nevin's.
107. *Mystical Presence,* p. 102n. Emphases mine.

a religion that drifts off into disembodied abstraction. In contrast to this, he argued for a greater attention to "life," by which he meant here the full range of religious and liturgical practices, and especially the practice of the eucharist. Union with Christ does not occur without engagement of the whole person, which requires external practice as well as rational thought. This concern of Nevin's continues Calvin's own conviction that God uses both audible words and visible and tangible symbols to engraft humanity into the body of Christ.

Although Nevin and Hodge lack Calvin's explicit reference to the balance of Word and sacrament, they, like Calvin (and Turretin), vigorously argued about the role of faith in the eucharist. They agreed that faith is necessary for the effective working of the sacrament, but they differed sharply in their understanding of how important it is. According to Nevin, the most important thing to bear in mind is the objectivity of the sacramental power: "The virtue which it possesses is not put into it by the faith of the worshiper in the first place, to be taken out of it again by the same faith, in the same form. It is not imagined of course in the case that the ordinance can have any virtue *without* faith, that it can confer grace in a purely mechanical way. . . . Still faith does not properly clothe the sacrament with its power. It is the condition of its efficacy for the communicant, but not the principle of the power itself."[108] Faith is indispensable, but is simply a receptacle for the power of the eucharist, which is the work of the Spirit.

Hodge, by contrast, was much more concerned to emphasize the role of faith in uniting the believer with Christ. According to Hodge, the proper Reformed doctrine holds that "feeding on the body and blood of Christ" means receiving Christ in the soul by faith and through the working of the Holy Spirit.[109] He was concerned that Nevin's doctrine began to look like *ex opere operato:* the doctrine that the sacraments work on their own, even without faith. Hodge did not deny the objective power of the eucharist; indeed, Hodge insisted that the efficacy of the sacrament is "solely in the attending influence of the Holy Ghost."[110] Yet because he was so concerned about Nevin's close identification of Christ with the church and sacraments, Hodge

---

108. *Mystical Presence*, p. 57.
109. Hodge, review of *Mystical Presence*, p. 246.
110. Hodge, review of *Mystical Presence*, p. 258.

sought to emphasize another dimension of Calvin's theology of the eucharist: the element of faith.

On this point, Nevin and Hodge both echoed Calvin, but Calvin at different moments of his argument. Hodge echoed the Calvin who was concerned about the idolatry of the material elements, the Calvin who claimed that the sacraments had no effect without some "taste of faith."[111] Nevin, more concerned about the arrogance of human reason that claims to understand what is going on at the table, held more closely to Calvin's insistence on God's objective action in the Supper. Calvin himself battled both of these misunderstandings, claiming that the eucharist must be received by faith to be effective, but that faith itself is not the effective power of the eucharist. Nevin and Hodge differed in their analysis of the central problem, and so they differed as to which side of Calvin's balance they retrieved.

Word, sacrament, faith, Spirit: for Calvin, all of these were oriented toward establishing a union of the believer and Christ. Nevin and Hodge agreed that union with Christ was the purpose of the Lord's Supper, and they agreed that the Spirit is what accomplishes this union, but they described it in different ways. Furthermore, the theme of "union with Christ" does not appear as central to Hodge's understanding as it was to Nevin's. Nevin began his entire treatise with the claim that "Christianity is grounded in the living union of the believer with the person of Christ; and this great fact is emphatically concentrated in the mystery of the Lord's Supper."[112] Union with Christ is the basis of Christianity, and the Lord's Supper is the most important Christian institution contributing to that union. There could hardly be a stronger claim for the centrality of the eucharist in Christian life. Moreover, Nevin continued, union with Christ is not simply common human existence,[113] nor simply moral or legal union,[114] nor union with only part of Christ's life.[115] Nevin insisted that union with Christ is union with the whole incarnation, both humanity and divinity. In this he stood against the popular "Puritan" view that we cannot par-

---

111. *Institutes* 4.17.33.
112. *Mystical Presence*, p. 47.
113. *Mystical Presence*, p. 51.
114. *Mystical Presence*, pp. 51-53.
115. *Mystical Presence*, pp. 53-54.

ticipate in Christ's humanity "except in the way of remembering what was endured in it for our salvation."[116]

Unlike Calvin, Nevin did not anchor his arguments for "mystical union" on the freedom of God or the work of the Holy Spirit, but on the incarnation of Jesus Christ. But like Calvin, he was concerned above all to combat the idea that the union was in any sense a human accomplishment. It was God's work, God's gift. And if the sacramental union is understood as God's work rather than our own, then surely we must attend to the physical and verbal details of the eucharistic event to discern how that union is transpiring.

Hodge also talked about union with Christ as the purpose of the eucharist. He even concurred with Nevin that

> [t]his union was always represented as a real union, not merely imaginary nor simply moral, nor arising from the mere reception of the benefits which Christ has procured. We receive Christ him-

---

116. *Mystical Presence*, p. 118. Nevin argued that our union with Christ's humanity does not mean union with material particles, but with a more general "law" of his human nature. He criticized Calvin (and, by implication, Zwingli) for insisting too strongly on the local presence of Christ in heaven rather than distinguishing between mere material particles and the "organic law" which is the true principle of life, and which is not bound to a particular place (see pp. 147ff.). He then went on to criticize Calvin's resolution of the problem, which was to rely on the power of the Holy Spirit to unite things separated by space (a resolution that Hodge argued was essential to the Reformed doctrine). Nevin affirmed that the Spirit was responsible for uniting the believer with Christ, but he objected that Calvin's formulation placed too much emphasis on the local, material body of Christ in heaven as the body to which the believer is joined. This, Nevin charged, was "confused, and brings to mind no proper satisfaction." Better to recognize that we participate in Christ's full humanity as part of his "generic life" rather than his individual personal life (pp. 151f.). This interpretation grew out of Nevin's appropriation of German idealistic philosophy, which distinguished between universal ideals and particular manifestations. Christ's "generic life" is the universal ideal; his incarnation redeemed, in principle, the whole of humanity. Though some contemporary theologians will criticize the influence of German idealism on Nevin's thought, his proposal is intriguing in its recognition that material particles themselves do not constitute the life of the body, and hence cannot be life-giving. He was reaching for something more basic, which he called the "organic law," to define what vivifies the body and makes it a coherent whole. This, he claimed, made it possible to maintain a real union with Christ's full person: humanity and divinity.

self, and are in Christ, united to him by the indwelling of his Spirit and by a living faith.[117]

The chief difference between Hodge and Nevin with regard to union with Christ is that Hodge located the union in the work of the Holy Spirit, while Nevin located it in our participation in Christ's very nature — which is accomplished by the Spirit.[118] Union is through the Spirit, argued Hodge, not direct participation in Christ's human life. Union is real participation in Christ's life, countered Nevin, which is by the power of the Spirit.[119] What difference does this make? For Hodge, even though the union between believer and Christ is real, its connection to the living embodied event of eucharist is tenuous. Union is established by the Holy Spirit and by faith, and this union can occur with or without the sacramental action. As Hodge himself asserted, there is no special gift in the eucharist, so the sacrament is not necessary to form the believer's faith or to engraft one into the body of Christ. This is a far cry from the union portrayed by Nevin, who insisted that in order to unite with Christ, one must participate in his ongoing life, communicated by the church and its sacraments. This view of union takes the concrete event of eucharist far more seriously as the medium through which the triune God works to bring people to Christ.

Reflecting on the fierce debate between Hodge and Nevin, historian E. Brooks Holifield notes that their sacramental disagreement illustrates a broader difference in their approaches to Reformed theology in general:

> While remaining with the Reformed tradition, Nevin demonstrated a willingness to accept categories of continuity that at times approximated the Roman Catholic tradition: continuity be-

---

117. Hodge, review of *Mystical Presence,* p. 229.

118. See Hodge, review of *Mystical Presence,* pp. 255 and 266-70.

119. Hodge criticized Nevin for inadequate pneumatology, charging that he identified the Holy Spirit so closely with the "theanthropic nature of Christ" that he did violence to the doctrine of the Trinity. (See Hodge, pp. 277f.) Nevin, for his part, criticized Calvin's appeal to the Holy Spirit as that which unites believers with the ascended body of Christ, claiming that this undermined full appreciation of our participation in Christ's humanity and also drives a wedge between the Spirit and Christ in a way that is not helpful. (See *Mystical Presence,* pp. 148, 150-51.)

tween creation and redemption, between the divine and human natures of Christ, between the first Adam and the second, and between the visible Church with its efficacious means of grace and the ideal communion of true saints. Charles Hodge, on the other hand, carried almost to its logical terminus another pattern present within the Reformed tradition: the impulse to accent discontinuity, in various ways, as the prevailing theological category.[120]

This analysis coheres with the particular observations I have made above. Nevin emphasizes continuity between the historic Christ and the church as Christ's continuing life in the world, between body and soul in human nature, and between the divine and human natures of Christ, while Hodge worries about too much continuity between Christ and the church, between the material and the spiritual dimensions of human nature, and between the human and divine natures of Christ.

This debate between Nevin and Hodge shows the continuing struggle in Reformed eucharistic theology three centuries after Calvin. Nevin tried to counter a prevailing emphasis on intelligible doctrine with a strong focus on sacrament as well as a more embodied understanding of mystical union. Hodge and Nevin each asserted one part of Calvin's approach to faith as a necessary element in the eucharist. Their different emphases grew out of different analyses of the theological issues of their day. But Nevin's description of the problem of "rationalistic heresy" resembles more closely one problem in our own day: too much emphasis on right doctrine, and insufficient respect for the power of the sacramental action as a means of divine work. To be sure, the contemporary problem is more subtle than Nevin's statement of the situation in his time, when "real presence of the whole Christ in the Lord's Supper, under any form, is counted a hard saying, not to be endured by human reason, and contrary to God's word."[121] In our time, people are less concerned to deny "real presence" as an affront to human reason, and yet many tend to think of articulated doctrine as prior to, or at least a necessary condition for, divine action.

---

120. E. Brooks Holifield, "Mercersburg, Princeton, and the South: The Sacramental Controversy in the Nineteenth Century," *Journal of Presbyterian History* 54 (1976): 239-40.

121. *Mystical Presence*, p. 103.

Conclusion

As this brief and selective exploration of Calvin and the Reformed tradition suggests, there is within this Protestant stream a strong appreciation for the event-character of the eucharist itself. Calvin and Nevin were particularly attentive to the ways in which a full appreciation of humanity, both ours and Christ's, requires that we regard the eucharist as more than the enactment of propositional statements. Calvin, in addition, described God's sovereignty in such a way that it promotes rather than inhibits divine involvement with creation, including sacramental objects and actions.

To be sure, there are also themes within this tradition that complicate an appreciation of the way God works in and through the eucharist. For instance, one question that has been debated since the time of Calvin is what role faith plays in the effectiveness of the sacrament. On the one hand, Calvin and Nevin both affirmed that faith is a necessary posture of receptivity within the worshiper. It enables the believer to receive the gift of God's grace offered through the bread and wine. The eucharistic elements do not work in some magical way to convey grace without the openness of the worshiper. But Turretin and Hodge described faith in a rather different manner. In the work of these theologians, faith became closely allied with doctrine, and it upstaged partaking of the physical sacrament as the way of uniting with Christ. Their view that there was no "special gift" in the eucharist, coupled with the implication that faith stands over against the church as a critical principle, rather than being nourished in and through the church, has contributed to a Reformed tendency to regard the eucharist as a secondary acting out of doctrine rather than a primary event of holy encounter. As a result, it has diminished Calvin's robust sense of the sacrament as a "means of grace," as a site of divine activity.

By reclaiming Calvin and Nevin's appreciation for God's work in and through the eucharist, the Reformed tradition today can use its own resources to respond to a contemporary problem: the characterization of liturgy in general and the eucharist in particular as merely human action, secondary to the careful articulation of right beliefs. This strand within Reformed theology can also learn from and be strengthened by some of the theological claims within the field of liturgical theology.

CHAPTER 2

Lex Orandi, Lex Credendi:
Resources from Liturgical Theology

Calvin, despite all his cautions about idolatry, had a firm respect for the eucharist as an event in which the triune God promises to meet people. The triune God is not only free from material creation, but free for active engagement with creation. As the Holy Spirit, God works to unite people with Christ in the eucharist. And this cannot happen without visible and tangible signs; hearing alone is insufficient to communicate God to human nature. Though later Reformed theologians such as Turretin and Hodge muted Calvin's emphasis on the balance of Word and sacrament, this early insistence that God works through symbolic objects and actions resurfaced in the work of John Williamson Nevin, who said that "nothing less than . . . a real participation of [Christ's] living person is involved always in the right use of the Lord's Supper."[1] So though not uniform, there is a recurrent recognition within the Reformed tradition that the eucharist is an important site of God's activity.

Many of these themes resonate with the claims of contemporary liturgical theologians, who focus on the way liturgy shapes doctrine. Even more strongly than most Reformed theologians, liturgical theologians insist that God works through liturgical action to form faith and unite people to God's own self. Yet liturgical theologians do not make this claim naïvely. As Don Saliers puts it, liturgy is (or may be)

---

1. John Williamson Nevin, *The Mystical Presence: A Vindication of the Reformed or Calvinistic Doctrine of the Holy Eucharist* (originally published in Philadelphia: J. B. Lippincott & Co., 1846; reprinted in Eugene, Oregon: Wipf & Stock, 2000), p. 31.

"*both* anthropological rite *and* divine self-manifestation."[2] Liturgy is holy encounter, but it is also a profoundly human activity. By trying to balance attention to God's activity in the liturgy and attention to raw anthropological detail, liturgical theologians provide a helpful model for the present project.

The field of liturgical theology has particularly flourished in the last few decades of this century, as a result of growing interest in historic liturgies and in the connection between worship and ecclesiology. Alexander Schmemann, Orthodox theologian and a major figure in contemporary liturgical theology, attributed the growth of this field to the "discovery of worship as the life of the Church, the public act which eternally actualizes the nature of the Church as the Body of Christ."[3] He defined liturgical theology as "the elucidation of the meaning of worship," by which he meant not mere symbolic explanation of the parts of worship, but articulation of the theological basis of the church's entire liturgical tradition.[4] Liturgical theology presents the theological meaning manifested in liturgical action. More recently, David Fagerberg has described liturgical theology as the theology that emerges in the liturgical action itself, "the meaning epiphanized in the ritual structure."[5] Although I accept Fagerberg's definition of liturgical theology as properly referring to that theology which comes to being in actual liturgies, I will use "liturgical theology" as a shorthand way of referring both to this primary theology and to secondary reflections on it such as Aidan Kavanagh's *On Liturgical Theology* and Gordon Lathrop's trilogy *Holy Things, Holy People,* and *Holy Ground.*[6]

---

2. Don Saliers, lecture in doctoral seminar on liturgical theology, Emory University, spring 1995.

3. Alexander Schmemann, *Introduction to Liturgical Theology,* trans. Ashleigh Moorhouse (London: The Faith Press, 1966), p. 12.

4. Schmemann, *Introduction to Liturgical Theology,* p. 14.

5. David Fagerberg, *What Is Liturgical Theology? A Study in Methodology* (Collegeville, Minn.: Liturgical Press, 1992), p. 180. Fagerberg devotes his entire book to defining liturgical theology proper, as distinct from theology *of* worship, theology *from* worship, and secondary reflections on liturgical theology's meaning and method. For an outline of these four approaches, see Fagerberg, pp. 11-12.

6. Aidan Kavanagh, *On Liturgical Theology,* The Hale Memorial Lectures of Seabury-Western Theological Seminary, 1981 (Collegeville, Minn.: Liturgical Press, 1984). Gordon Lathrop, *Holy Things: A Liturgical Theology* (Minneapolis: Fortress Press, 1993); *Holy People: A Liturgical Ecclesiology* (Minneapolis: Fortress Press, 1999); *Holy Ground: A*

Lex Orandi and *Lex Credendi*

One of the epigrams of contemporary liturgical theologians comes from the fifth-century writer Prosper of Aquitaine: *ut legem credendi lex statuat supplicandi,* often cited simply as *lex orandi, lex credendi.* Scholars have disagreed sharply over the past few decades about how to construe this ancient clause. Some, like Kavanagh and his student David Fagerberg, translate Prosper's words straightforwardly: "The law of praying (*lex supplicandi* or *lex orandi*) establishes (*statuat*) the law of believing (*legem credendi*)."[7] Construed in this manner, the relationship of praying and believing is unidirectional; we do not believe and then worship, but we encounter God in worship, and therefore we believe. As Kavanagh puts it, "Our reception of God's Word is subordinated to the presentation of that Word to us in the act of its being revealed and proclaimed to us. Belief is always consequent upon encounter with the Source of the grace of faith."[8] Secondary theology, then, as presentation of belief, follows from worship. This does not mean that theology can have no effect on worship, but simply that it is not the foundation of worship. Kavanagh goes on to say that to reverse this order, to make the law of worship subordinate to the law of belief (or theology), would destroy the movement of revelation:

> It was a Presence, not faith, which drew Moses to the burning bush, and what happened there was a revelation, not a seminar. It was a Presence, not faith, which drew the disciples to Jesus, and what happened then was not an educational program but his revelation to them of himself as the long-promised Anointed One, the redeeming because reconciling Messiah-Christos. Their lives, like that of Moses, were changed radically by that encounter with a Presence which upended all their ordinary expectations. Their descendants in faith have been adjusting to that change ever

Liturgical Cosmology (Minneapolis: Fortress Press, 2003). For an introduction to the sources of liturgical theology, see *Primary Sources of Liturgical Theology: A Reader,* ed. Dwight W. Vogel (Collegeville, Minn.: Liturgical Press, 2000).

7. J.-P. Migne, *Patrologia Latina,* vol. 51: col. 209. Fagerberg cites Prosper's epigram in support of his argument that liturgy is the "ontological condition" for theology. Fagerberg, *What Is Liturgical Theology?* p. 17.

8. Kavanagh, *On Liturgical Theology,* p. 91.

since, drawn into assembly by that same Presence, finding there always the troublesome upset of change in their lives of faith to which they must adjust still. Here is where their lives are regularly being constituted and reconstituted under grace. Which is why *lex supplicandi legem statuat credendi.*[9]

Kavanagh equates the liturgy here with encounter with God, implying that what happens on a Sunday morning is equivalent to Moses' encounter with the great "I AM" in the burning bush.

This understanding of the relationship of worship and faith builds on the earlier work of Schmemann, who writes persuasively about the need to recover the early church's sense of *lex orandi* as the ground for *lex credendi.* Such a close relationship may well have characterized the early churches, given the evidence that patristic writers often appealed to liturgical practice to support their theological points. However, the situation gradually changed, especially in the West. *Lex credendi* was increasingly conducted without appeal to *lex orandi.* Theology, as "the orderly and consistent presentation, explication, and defense of the Church's faith," came to identify faith with propositional statements.[10] No longer was faith identified primarily with the experience of the worshiping community. According to Schmemann, this was in contrast to the Eastern churches, for whom faith continued to be "the total and living experience of the Church."[11] Schmemann bemoans this shift in Western understanding, insisting that

> the faith which founds the Church and by which she lives is not mere assent to a "doctrine," but her living relationship to certain events: the Life, Death, Resurrection and Glorification of Jesus Christ, His Ascension to heaven, the descent of the Holy Spirit on the last and great day of Pentecost — a relationship which makes

9. Kavanagh, *On Liturgical Theology,* p. 92.

10. Alexander Schmemann, "Liturgy and Theology," *Greek Orthodox Theological Review* 17, no. 1 (1972): 89. Turretin is a good example of this tendency, but note also that the Western tradition is not uniform on this; Nevin presents a clear counterexample of a Western Reformed theologian who took seriously the way the church is "epiphanized" in the eucharist (though this is Schmemann's language, not Nevin's).

11. Schmemann, "Liturgy and Theology," p. 89.

her a constant "witness" and "participant" of these events, of their saving, redeeming, life-giving and life-transfiguring reality.[12]

Theology, according to this view, is no independent scientific discipline that leads to knowledge of God through rational argument. It is description, in orderly and consistent manner, of that which the church experiences in liturgy, in *lex orandi*.

This is the most radical interpretation of *lex orandi, lex credendi,* and it is certainly open to the criticism that worship is not the same thing as the revelation to Moses or the disciples' encounter with Jesus. The anti-idolatry strand in Reformed theology, while it has at times handicapped a full appreciation of the work of God in worship, is yet useful in maintaining a critical distance between revelation and liturgy. Liturgy is not God.

Paul Marshall has offered a stinging critique of Kavanagh's and Fagerberg's (but not Schmemann's) understanding of *lex orandi, lex credendi* along these lines in his 1995 article "Reconsidering 'Liturgical Theology': Is There a *Lex Orandi* for All Christians?"[13] In it, he argues that Kavanagh and Fagerberg present "the liturgy" as simply a given that "the people" receive passively, rather than actively participating in the formation and critique of that liturgy. This strand of liturgical theology, according to Marshall, depicts the relationship between *lex orandi* and *lex credendi* as a one-way street, from the divinely given liturgy to the human response of believing. This perpetuates a view of the liturgy that is fixed, authoritarian, and hierarchical. In the context of this critique, Marshall presents a careful exegesis of Prosper's famous dictum in which he argues that Prosper himself never intended to posit liturgical action as the single norm that establishes Christian believing. Instead, this line occurs near the end of a lengthy argument on the subject of Christian believing. Prosper's overall point, arguing against semi-Pelagianism, is that believing is a gift from God, not a human achievement. In the first six chapters of the treatise, Prosper cites papal teachings and the Council of Carthage to support his view; only then does he turn to the example of the lit-

12. Schmemann, "Liturgy and Theology," p. 90.
13. Paul V. Marshall, "Reconsidering 'Liturgical Theology': Is There a *Lex Orandi* for All Christians?" *Studia Liturgica* 25 (1995): 129-51.

urgy, and particularly the bidding prayers. Marshall translates the passage as follows:

> In addition, let us look at the sacred testimony of priestly interces-
> sions which have been transmitted from the apostles and which
> are uniformly celebrated throughout the world and in every cath-
> olic church . . . so that the law [or rule or pattern] of supplicating
> [not the more general *orandi*, "praying"] may establish [or con-
> firm] the law [or rule or pattern] of believing [not "the faith"].[14]

What Prosper sees in the "testimony of priestly intercessions" is evidence that the whole church believes what he is arguing: that we have
to receive faith from God as a gift. Priests would not be praying for
people to receive this unless it were a gift of grace. The point with regard to *lex orandi* (or, as Marshall reminds us, *lex supplicandi*) is that
Prosper appeals to universal liturgical practice not because it is the
only source, or even the first source, for theological reflection, but because it is a reliable source that demonstrates the broad apostolic
Christian faith.

Liturgical scholar Mary Collins has offered a similar critique of the
use of the formulation *lex orandi legem statuat credendi* in liturgical theology. As Collins points out, the claim that the rule of worship establishes the rule of faith (and therefore theology) has often focused on
the objectivity and uniformity of the liturgy, ignoring or denigrating
any regional variations.[15] The liturgy presents the mystery of salvation
as revealed in the death and resurrection of Jesus Christ: this is the
wondrous claim made by liturgical theologians. This is the content of
the *lex orandi* which establishes the *lex credendi*. The problem is that
there seems little room for particularity or subjectivity in this vision of
the church's *lex orandi* as a single *lex*. And yet, as Collins notes, "Local,
regional and cultural particularity in expression are every bit as significant for understanding the church's liturgy and the church's belief as
objectivity in content and structure."[16] Like Marshall, she is concerned

---

14. Marshall, "Reconsidering 'Liturgical Theology,'" p. 140.

15. Mary Collins, "Critical Questions for Liturgical Theology," in *Worship: Renewal to Practice* (Washington, D.C.: Pastoral Press, 1987): 116-17.

16. Collins, "Critical Questions for Liturgical Theology," p. 117.

for the liturgical practices that are disregarded by the appeal to a universal *lex orandi*.[17]

Mediating voices in this debate about the meaning of Prosper's phrase are Geoffrey Wainwright and Kevin Irwin.[18] Both scholars point out that Prosper's dictum did not presume liturgical fixity, nor did it draw on liturgical practice as the sole or chief norm for doctrine (contra Kavanagh and Fagerberg). Rather, they agree on the more modest claim that "the liturgy manifests the church's faith" and that it is "a theological source to the degree that it is founded on Scripture and is the expression of a praying Church."[19] Both Wainwright and Irwin go on to demonstrate that this sort of appeal to liturgical practice in theological debate was common in the patristic era (a point that Marshall neglects to make). Wainwright then skillfully presents the "interplay" between *lex orandi* and *lex credendi* throughout the history of Christian theologizing, arguing that at times the appeal to liturgical practice has been helpful, and at other times (particularly in the Protestant Reformation), church leaders have appropriately ap-

17. Teresa Berger offers a similar critique from an explicitly feminist perspective in her essay "Prayers and Practices of Women: Lex Orandi Reconfigured," in *Women, Ritual, and Liturgy*, ed. Susan K. Roll, Annette Esser, et al., Yearbook of the European Society of Women in Theological Research (Louvain: Peeters, 2001), pp. 63-77. Berger points out that theologians who appeal to the principle of *lex orandi, lex credendi* "have occluded the distinct shape of the prayers and practices of women" (p. 63). Therefore, she calls for "continuing and sustained reflection on a feminist reconfiguring of *lex orandi*," paying particular attention to women's prayers and practices (pp. 65-66).

18. Geoffrey Wainwright, *Doxology: The Praise of God in Worship, Doctrine, and Life: A Systematic Theology* (New York: Oxford University Press, 1980), pp. 224-27. Wainwright's entire discussion of *lex orandi, lex credendi* extends from pp. 218 to 283. Kevin W. Irwin, "Lex Orandi, Lex Credendi — Origins and Meaning: State of the Question," *Liturgical Ministry* 11 (Spring 2002): 57-69. See also Paul de Clerck, "'Lex orandi, lex credendi': Sens original et avatars historiques d'un adage équivoque," *Questions Liturgiques* 59 (1978): 193-212, translated into English as "'Lex orandi, lex credendi': The Original Sense and Historical Avatars of an Equivocal Adage," *Studia Liturgica* 24 (1994): 178-200. For a discussion of the points of disagreement between Kavanagh and Wainwright, see Kevin Irwin, *Liturgical Theology: A Primer* (Collegeville, Minn.: Liturgical Press, 1990), pp. 46-47. On this discussion, see also E. Byron Anderson and Bruce T. Morrill, "The Prophetic Challenge: Introduction," in *Liturgy and the Moral Self: Humanity at Full Stretch Before God* (Collegeville, Minn.: Liturgical Press, 1998), pp. 4f.

19. Irwin, "Lex Orandi, Lex Credendi," p. 59.

pealed to church doctrine to correct malformed worship practices. *Lex orandi* and *lex credendi* are mutually formative, and we need not argue for one as permanent trump card over the other.

Having said these things, I concur with Wainwright that the principle *ut legem credendi lex statuat supplicandi* (and perhaps even Kavanagh's stark interpretation of it) offers a helpful corrective to the Reformed Protestant tradition at this time. For a Christian stream that has so often maintained the priority of doctrine over practice, it is important to recognize that participation in liturgical action over time deeply forms faith. The worshiping community encounters God in Word and sacrament, and that encounter shapes believing.[20] In response to Collins's appropriate critique of liturgical theology, I argue that Prosper of Aquitaine's ancient statement need not rule out attention to particularity and subjectivity. Surely it is possible to acknowledge that the way we worship founds the way we believe without going on to claim that only one form of worship counts as *lex orandi*. Our task is then to explore in detail the actual liturgical celebrations of a community in order to discover what *lex credendi* is being established by the local *lex orandi*.[21]

---

20. Wainwright says, "the Protestant practice of doctrine needs to recover a more explicit doxological dimension. The liturgical perspective can help Protestant theology in this regard" (*Doxology*, p. 219). James Kay has followed up on this suggestion in his essay in the festschrift for Wainwright, "The Lex Orandi in Recent Protestant Theology," in *Ecumenical Theology in Worship, Doctrine, and Life: Essays Presented to Geoffrey Wainwright on His Sixtieth Birthday*, ed. David S. Cunningham, Ralph del Colle, and Lucas Lamadrid (New York: Oxford University Press, 1999), pp. 11-23. In the essay, Kay explores the *lex orandi* as a source for Christian doctrine in the work of Thomas Oden, Alister McGrath, John Leith, Robert Jenson, and Christopher Morse. For an interesting reflection on the difference between *lex orandi, lex credendi* and the tradition of doctrinal preaching in the Church of Scotland, see Donald Baillie, "The Preaching of Christian Doctrine," in *The Theology of the Sacraments and Other Papers* (New York: Charles Scribner's Sons, 1957), pp. 142ff. Baillie does not suggest that the liturgical maxim is opposed to the Reformed tradition; indeed, he suggests a need to integrate preaching more fully with the sacraments and the observance of the liturgical year, implicitly acknowledging the integral relationship between doctrine and practice.

21. But again, it is important not to focus so much on particularity that one ignores the common shape that has characterized Christian worship from the earliest days. Gordon Lathrop nicely balances attention to common things with appreciation for local variation when he says, "Worship is not and ought not to be the same everywhere . . . [local churches] are always the catholic church dwelling *in this particular*

With regard to Reformed eucharistic theology in particular, this principle challenges the view propounded by Turretin and Hodge: that doctrine precedes the church and sacraments, or that right eucharistic practice is established by prior careful theological reflection. These theologians would likely be quite comfortable asserting that the *lex credendi* establishes *lex orandi,* that right worship depends on prior understanding of doctrine. And in certain historical contexts, as Wainwright reminds us, attention to doctrine as a source for reforming worship is appropriate. But liturgical theologians remind us of the opposite movement as well: theological reflection is deeply formed by the eucharistic practices of a particular community. Anticipating the language of ritual studies, we might say that what the eucharist "does" is to form relationships and shape meaning. Meaning does not exist independently prior to practice. *Lex credendi* does not exist prior to *lex orandi*. Before any normative judgments about eucharistic practices can be made, therefore, one must first live and worship with a community and observe how their practices form the basis for what they believe about God, themselves, and the world. One must learn their *lex orandi*.[22]

Liturgy as Primary Theology

It is not sufficient, however, simply to assert that the law of worship establishes or shapes the law of faith, for this still implies that worship and articulated faith are two different activities. Recent scholars of liturgical theology go on to say that not only does worship found theology; it *is* theology. As noted earlier, David Fagerberg defines liturgical theology as that meaning which is "epiphanized" in the ritual struc-

---

place. But they are also *the catholic church* dwelling here" (*Holy People,* p. 114). *Lex orandi* comprises both the local and the universal, both particularity and catholicity.

22. Of course, *lex orandi* must always also be understood in the context of a larger tradition of praying and reflecting. Worship is never a pristine "first act," but is a part of a messy history of "dubious practice and half-conceived reflection" (private communication, Stan Hall, May 2000). So in considering the eucharistic practices of a given community, one must also consider the history of practice and reflection that forms the context of that community. This is the approach I have taken in chapter four.

ture of worship.[23] Liturgy is not simply raw unformed data that true theologians must systematize to produce meaning. Liturgical action itself produces meaning. It can thus be called "primary theology."

Many scholars have pointed out that theology and liturgy have for too long been regarded as separate activities, the first having to do with reason and the second with emotion.[24] This separation diminishes both enterprises; theology becomes the exclusive domain of professional academics who gravely explain the truths of the faith to untutored believers, and liturgy shrinks to little more than a weekly opportunity to celebrate ourselves and our place in the world before going off to brunch at the country club. This separation of theology and liturgy perpetuates the false assumption that the purpose of worship is to express our ideas and feelings about God rather than to encounter the living One who created us, redeemed us, and fills us with new life. The preacher and congregation, according to this view, need to do their theological work first, in order that the people may worship correctly. But this is not only backwards, as implied by the principle *legem credendi lex statuat supplicandi;* it posits a separation where there should be none. It ignores the theological work that goes on every time the people assemble to pray, to listen, and to share a meal. What is theology, after all, if not the use of words *(logos)* to inch toward understanding the relationships among God *(theos),* world, and humanity?[25] And what is liturgy if not an attempt to understand and enact those very relationships? Liturgy, as search for and enactment of meaning, is genuinely theological action.

Put simply, theology can be defined as "knowledge of God." Such knowledge emerges in the activity of addressing and being addressed by God, which transpires in liturgy. Liturgy is not the only place where this occurs, but it is certainly a significant place where Christians have trusted God to speak to and to hear the prayers of God's gathered peo-

23. Fagerberg, *What Is Liturgical Theology?* p. 180.

24. This is the situation that Alexander Schmemann describes as the central problem in "Liturgy and Theology" and in his introductory chapter to *Introduction to Liturgical Theology.* For more on this topic, see also Kavanagh, *On Liturgical Theology,* pp. 82f. and Fagerberg, *What Is Liturgical Theology?* pp. 13 and 194-98.

25. See Fagerberg, *What Is Liturgical Theology?* p. 10. For a similar emphasis on understanding as the goal of liturgy, and that which marks it as theology, see Robert Taft, "Liturgy as Theology," *Worship* 56, no. 2 (March 1982): 113-17.

ple. Secondary reflection on this knowledge grows out of the primary activity of worshiping God. And further, the activity of worshiping itself, as intelligible word and gesture, constitutes theology.[26]

Aidan Kavanagh describes a dialectical structure of liturgy that illumines the way in which liturgy is theology. As he says, in liturgy the assembly is brought to the edge of chaos in a holy encounter with God. As a result, the people are deeply changed, and "deep change will affect their next liturgical act, howsoever slightly. To detect that change in the subsequent liturgical act will be to discover where theology has passed, rather as physics detects atomic particles in tracks of their passage through a liquid medium. . . . It is the *adjustment* which is theological in all this. I hold that it is theology being born, theology in the first instance. It is what tradition has called *theologia prima.*"[27] Encounter — change — adjustment: this is the pattern of the liturgy. *Theologia prima,* primary theology, is the adjustment to the change caused by an encounter between the assembly and God.

Central to the understanding of liturgy as primary theology is its corporate nature. *Theologia prima* is not done by private individuals, but publicly, in the community of faith. The liturgical assembly is a "theological corporation," as Kavanagh puts it.[28] And as Gordon Lathrop says, "Primary liturgical theology is the communal meaning of the liturgy exercised by the gathering itself. The assembly uses combinations of words and signs to speak of God."[29] This too is in contrast to the common understanding of theology as a solitary activity, done perhaps by someone who goes to worship regularly, but certainly not done by the whole community. This naming of liturgy as primary theology relativizes the distinctions between ordained and non-ordained Christians, encouraging ordained leaders to honor the very real

26. Based on a lecture by Don Saliers, Ph.D. seminar, January 12, 1995.

27. Kavanagh, *On Liturgical Theology,* pp. 73-74.

28. Aidan Kavanagh, "Response [to Geoffrey Wainwright]: Primary Theology and Liturgical Act," *Worship* 57 (July 1983): 309-24. Cited in Fagerberg, *What Is Liturgical Theology?* p. 18. Kavanagh also lists as one of the chief characteristics of primary theology the fact that it is "communitarian," not done by a lonely scholar but by a gathered assembly (*On Liturgical Theology,* p. 89).

29. Gordon Lathrop, *Holy Things: A Liturgical Theology* (Minneapolis: Fortress Press, 1993), p. 5.

theologizing that goes on among the people, and prodding the congregation to recognize the import of what they do week after week.

How does this notion of liturgy as *theologia prima* advance the understanding of the eucharist in the Reformed tradition? As with the rest of liturgical activity, it focuses on the eucharist as a primary encounter with God, rather than secondary expression. If we take Kavanagh's dialectical pattern and apply it to the eucharist in particular, we can say that at the table the assembly meets the living God and is altered by the encounter. In adjusting to this change, the assembly commits an act of theology; in its very attempt to make sense of what just happened, the congregation gathered is already doing theological work. Part of this adjustment can be seen in the symbolic use of language: the congregation uses descriptions of God to address God. The assembly receives food and drink from the gracious God at table, and out of that transaction they learn to call on God as gracious.

A more specific example of theological adjustment may be helpful at this point. For three years in the 1990s, I worshiped with a Presbyterian congregation that celebrated communion once a month. For the first year, the tone of each communion service was about the same: the words emphasized joy and inclusiveness, but the performance was fairly somber and quiet. We all sat in our places while the bread and juice were passed down the rows. The movement was minimal, and few worshipers looked at each other as the elements were passed. Then, during the second year, the congregation worshiped in a neighboring Catholic church while our building was undergoing renovation. The shift in place necessitated a shift in the way we celebrated communion; rather than passing the trays of bread and tiny glasses of grape juice down the rows, we began processing down the aisles to receive the elements from the servers at the front of the sanctuary. Suddenly the mood was different. People looked at one another. They smiled. The servers and the partakers exchanged words over the bread and cup — something that had rarely happened before. The gathering took on the tone of a joyful celebration rather than a sober time of individual reflection. This was not due to the words, which had hardly changed from one location to the other. In Kavanagh's terms, the assembly met God in a new way in that celebration, which changed their relationship to the eucharist ever after. Without articulating an argument, the congregation adjusted to that change by coming to the table with greater

72

joy, understanding it as a jubilant feast rather than just a memorial meal. This adjustment was genuinely theological, though unplanned by any worship leader or academic theologian. If we regard liturgy in general and eucharist in particular as primary theology, then we open our eyes to these theological maneuvers of the congregation, honoring them as genuine responses to the encounter with the divine presence.

Descriptive and Normative Tasks
of Liturgical Theology

The two preceding claims — that the rule of worship establishes the rule of faith and that worship itself is primary theology — have brought us to a problem. All liturgy functions to form us in faith, and yet not all liturgy does this adequately. It is all very well to insist that liturgy is *theologia prima,* but what if the theology that is emerging there presents God as merely our personal guidance counselor, humanity as a collection of unrelated individuals who are each entitled to pursue our individual goals of happiness and wealth, and the world as our plaything to do with as we please? How does liturgical theology move from being simply descriptive to addressing normative concerns? How does praise become adequate to its object — namely, God?

If theology and liturgy are regarded as two separate enterprises, the answer seems obvious. Geoffrey Wainwright is one example of a theologian who takes worship seriously, but does not understand worship itself as theology. He presents theology and liturgy as two parallel phenomena, both emerging from tradition. Secondary theology thus can critique liturgy independently of liturgy's own theology. As Wainwright describes it, the theologian's task is to present doctrine, which is "a coherent intellectual expression of the Christian vision." This vision grows out of worship, but it also helps critique worship, improving or correcting it where necessary.[30] So while worship does shape doctrine, doctrine also influences worship, altering the structure when it has become problematic.[31]

Fagerberg and Kavanagh both criticize this move by Wainwright.

---

30. Wainwright, *Doxology,* p. 3.
31. See sections on "lex orandi" and "lex credendi" in *Doxology,* pp. 218-83.

Fagerberg points out that Wainwright seems to suggest that liturgy creates feelings that then influence the thinker/theologian. This is one instance of the modern tendency to regard liturgy as emotional and theology as rational. But liturgy does more than create feelings; it creates persons. Liturgy brings the community into being and creates attitudes toward the self, God, and the world. There is no independent place for "doctrine" to stand from which to critique liturgy, because doctrine itself rests on the foundation of liturgy.[32] But this returns us to the question of liturgical theology's normative task. How can we critique inadequate liturgy without having secondary theology operate independently of primary theology?

Fagerberg and Lathrop offer two different approaches to this question. Fagerberg distinguishes liturgy (that is, the style and protocol of worship) from *leitourgia* (the content of worship). "Liturgy" in this sense refers to the details of how to do worship properly: what colors the paraments should be, what clergy should wear, when people stand or sit, and so forth. It is the "how" of worship. True *leitourgia*, on the other hand, is the enactment of the world "as it was meant to be done."[33] It is, to use Kavanagh's terminology, the assembly's adjustment to the encounter with the holy. Of course, *leitourgia* has to do with actual liturgical action, but it encompasses more than that; *leitourgia* is both the encounter of the assembly with God and the assembly's adjustment to that encounter.[34] It is the "what" of worship.

Having made this distinction, Fagerberg goes on to argue that *leitourgia* can critique liturgy. There exists in *leitourgia* a fundamental logic that can be read and understood by all practitioners, even if they are not formally trained in theology. "*Leitourgia* is ordered, logical, grammatical, canonical, meaningful, deeply structured, and functions according to Tradition. As such, it is itself theological."[35] When one is formed over time by this *leitourgia*, one is equipped to judge for oneself when any particular liturgy is inadequate.

A problem with Fagerberg's proposal is that it is ambivalent with

32. See Fagerberg, *What Is Liturgical Theology?* pp. 102-32. But note also Kevin Irwin's defense of Wainwright in *Context and Text: Method in Liturgical Theology* (Collegeville, Minn.: Liturgical Press, 1994), pp. 15-16.

33. Kavanagh, cited by Fagerberg, *What Is Liturgical Theology?* p. 189.

34. See Fagerberg, *What Is Liturgical Theology?* p. 187.

35. Fagerberg, *What Is Liturgical Theology?* pp. 222-23.

regard to concrete liturgical action. On the one hand he lifts up concrete liturgy as that which forms persons and epiphanizes the encounter between God and humanity. But on the other hand, he says that not all worship is *leitourgia;* not all worship counts as primary theology. This is linked to the instrumentalization of worship: worship has become a means to an end, which is too often personal enrichment.[36] It is no longer holy encounter. But in separating so radically leitourgia from concrete liturgy, one is left wondering where we can find actual instances of *leitourgia.* What does it look like? Does it even exist anymore, or are we all lost in a sea of mere "worship" that is oriented to individual fulfillment? And if this be the case, is it not true that Fagerberg has committed the very error he seems intent on avoiding: using an abstraction *(leitourgia)* to judge concrete reality (worship)? He criticizes Wainwright and others for using secondary theology to critique liturgy, saying, "This is not liturgical theology proper because it does not research the liturgical act itself but instead treats, on a secondary level, a doctrine extracted (abstracted) from the action."[37] Has not Fagerberg himself come dangerously close to this same practice?[38]

Lathrop is more helpful in providing normative guidelines for liturgy drawn from within the liturgy itself. From analysis of ancient liturgies as well as liturgical practices of many Christian communions today, he proposes an underlying structural principle of all liturgy: the juxtaposition of strong symbols that are constantly being broken and made new. Holy things should be prominent in liturgical celebration, and they should be held always in tension with one another. These symbols should also be lifted up as simultaneously holy and not-holy. Christian symbols are at once "holy things for holy people" and not-holy, for "One is holy, one is Lord: Jesus Christ, to the glory of God."[39]

---

36. Fagerberg, *What Is Liturgical Theology?* p. 187.

37. Fagerberg, *What Is Liturgical Theology?* p. 183.

38. To be sure, the normative-descriptive ambiguity is always present in this kind of project. One cannot describe "liturgy" without forming some normative sense of what constitutes "real liturgy." The challenge is to admit one's normative judgments while remaining engaged as fully as possible in the descriptive task. Fagerberg initially commits himself to describing concrete liturgy, but later seems to allow his normative concerns to eclipse description without acknowledging this shift.

39. See Lathrop, *Holy Things,* p. 11. This liturgical response is one form of an ancient call to communion, which Lathrop discusses at length in *Holy Things,* chapter 5.

This principle guides Lathrop's "pastoral liturgical theology," which aims to reform liturgical patterns in order to allow the symbols to speak more clearly.[40]

In particular, he suggests that there is a deep structure evident in Christian worship throughout the world and throughout history: "a participating community together with its ministers gathered in song and prayer around the Scriptures read and preached, around the baptismal washing, enacted or remembered, and around the Holy Supper."[41] The people and the ministers, song and prayer, the Word read and preached, washing and meal: this is the ancient structure that has come down to us. These are not abstractions, but are actual local practices that characterize "most catholic churches throughout the twenty centuries of Christianity."[42] This ordo can be identified with Prosper's *lex orandi* because it is biblically based, firmly grounded in tradition, and ecumenically practiced today. This rule, emerging from liturgical practice itself, can then be used to critique any particular instance of liturgy. As Lathrop puts it, we can all ask one another, "Are Scriptures and preaching, *eucharistia* and eating and drinking, teaching and washing clear and central in your assemblies?"[43] This kind of liturgical criticism calls for symbols that are at once strong and broken; able to be read and understood by the assembly but also understood to point beyond themselves to the suffering Christ and suffering humanity.[44]

Unlike Wainwright, Lathrop draws criteria for worship from the liturgical shape itself rather than from an independent realm of doctrine. Unlike Fagerberg, he points to concrete liturgical actions as criteria, rather than creating an abstract concept floating above the complicated details of actual practice. In outlining this ordo, this *lex orandi*, Lathrop is able to critique specific instances of liturgical practice without departing from the realm of liturgy to do so.

---

40. Lathrop, *Holy Things*, p. 7.
41. Lathrop, *Holy People*, pp. 106-7.
42. Lathrop, *Holy People*, p. 107.
43. Lathrop, *Holy People*, p. 115.
44. See Lathrop, *Holy Things*, pp. 161-64.

Criticism and Self-Criticism of Liturgical Theology

With its emphasis on the deeply formative character of *lex orandi* and its further claim that liturgy constitutes primary theology, liturgical theology is a helpful lens for retrieving Calvin's emphasis on the real activity of God in the eucharist. At the same time, liturgical theologians acknowledge that not every instance of liturgical action is an adequate expression of the work of God, an acknowledgment that coheres with the critical stance of Reformed theology with regard to human actions and symbols. Gordon Lathrop is particularly helpful in balancing respect for the formative power of liturgy with principles drawn from *lex orandi* that can critique particular liturgical celebrations. But while its overarching principles are helpful, the field of liturgical theology has often been troubled by methodologies that fail to attend to the power of local liturgical practices. Two major trends within liturgical theology have contributed to this lack of attention to the local: an early preoccupation with texts, and a later reliance on structuralist analysis.

The first problem is the tendency of some liturgical theologians, like scholars in the older field of liturgical studies, to focus on texts to the exclusion of specific local practices. This is not surprising, since so many earlier liturgical theologians were trained in the discipline of liturgical history, which deals largely in textual sources. Kevin Irwin notes that "the seminal efforts in this century in liturgical theology emphasized the interpretation of texts."[45] A growing number of liturgical theologians are aware of the dangers of a narrowly textual approach to liturgy. Schmemann himself criticizes this tendency and emphasizes that liturgical theology is to examine the entire experience of liturgy, not just the texts. The Paschal Triduum, for instance, reveals "more about the 'doctrines' of Creation, Fall, Redemption, Death and Resurrection than all other *loci theologici* together; and, let me stress it, *not merely in the texts*, in the magnificent Byzantine hymnography, but precisely by the very 'experience' — ineffable yet illuminating — given during these days in their inner interdependence, in their nature; indeed as epiphany and revelation."[46]

45. Kevin Irwin, *Context and Text,* p. 53. As examples of this, Irwin cites especially Lambert Beauduin and M. Cappuyns, but see also his general comments on p. 32.
46. Schmemann, "Liturgy and Theology," p. 97. Emphasis mine.

Mary Collins in particular has noted the textual focus of early liturgical theologians and called for an expansion of methods within the field. As she says, "Only a small part of the work of contemporary liturgical study is done when the history of the officially revised liturgical books is set forward and the intended theological meaning exposed. . . . The most vast undertaking of contemporary liturgical studies is to attend to the actual local practice, the customary usage of particular churches."[47] Official texts alone do not constitute the entirety of liturgy; the peculiarities of performance must also be considered. Kevin Irwin agrees: "Liturgy is far more than texts. Liturgy is an enacted communal symbolic event with a number of constitutive elements and means of communication, including, but not restricted to, texts."[48] And Mark Searle also sounded the call for a new approach in liturgical theology, lamenting in 1992, "The study of liturgy has for the most part been the study of liturgical texts. . . . This is unfortunate, since what differentiates liturgy from other faith-expressions, such as preaching, poetry, iconography, and so on, is that it is essentially something that is what it is when it is carried out. It requires the physical presence of living bodies interacting in the same general space at the same time and passing through a series of prescribed motions. Liturgy is uniquely a matter of the body."[49]

In response to this criticism of the field's textual focus, more recent liturgical theologians have been moving to a new appreciation for concrete liturgical practices. Theodore Jennings pointed scholars in this direction in a 1987 article in which he suggested ways in which liturgical theology and ritual studies could enrich one another. Among other things, he said, "Liturgical theology may acquire significant new tools for the critical analysis of its object," for instance, development of the genre of the ethnographic report, development of a ritual taxonomy, and use of tools from structural linguistics and the study of ritual as

47. Mary Collins, "Ritual Symbols and the Ritual Process: The Work of Victor W. Turner," in *Worship: Renewal to Practice* (Washington, D.C.: Pastoral Press, 1987), p. 61.

48. Irwin, *Context and Text*, p. 32. He goes on to name this approach explicitly as a new method: "liturgy as event sets the framework for a new method in liturgical theology" (p. 53).

49. Mark Searle, "Ritual," in *The Study of Liturgy*, rev. ed., edited by Cheslyn Jones, Geoffrey Wainwright, Edward Yarnold, and Paul Bradshaw (New York: Oxford University Press, 1992), p. 56.

performance.[50] In all of these ways, he suggested, the field of ritual studies might help liturgical scholars to focus on concrete liturgical performances rather than relying solely on textual evidence. Reflecting this general move toward appreciation of liturgy as concrete practice, the editors of the 1992 revised edition of *The Study of Liturgy* chose to add an article on ritual, a subject that had not been addressed in the 1978 edition. Mark Searle proposed in that article that liturgical theologians should study liturgy *as ritual,* which is "to study liturgy . . . in its empirical reality as a species of significant human behavior."[51] Searle and his editors clearly saw the need to move toward appreciation of liturgy as "anthropological rite," to use Saliers's terminology, and not simply enactment of set texts.

Mary Collins had begun to borrow tools from ritual scholars even before Jennings and Searle wrote their articles. Like Jennings, she identifies two major approaches within the field of ritual studies that can be helpful to liturgical theologians: structural analysis (drawing especially on the work of Lévi-Strauss) and "situational analysis" (relying particularly on Victor Turner).[52] As I will discuss below, she notes problems with structuralism when it is used exclusively, but she acknowledges strengths in both approaches. Generally speaking, structuralism highlights similarities among rituals that appear to be widely divergent, and performance theory focuses on particularities within each ritual performance that make its meaning specific to its local time and place. Collins calls for a balance of the two methods to help liturgical theology appreciate both the "deep structure" that unites liturgies and the local differences in performance that shape meaning in particular ways.[53]

Another contemporary liturgical theologian who concentrates on concrete liturgical practices is Gordon Lathrop. His volumes *Holy Things, Holy People,* and *Holy Ground* deftly combine his traditional training in liturgical texts with an interest in actual liturgical perfor-

---

50. Theodore W. Jennings, Jr., "Ritual Studies and Liturgical Theology: An Invitation to Dialogue," *Journal of Ritual Studies* 1, no. 1 (1987): 43-45.

51. Mark Searle, "Ritual," in *The Study of Liturgy,* p. 52.

52. Collins, "Ritual Symbols and the Ritual Process," pp. 63-69. See also pp. 116-19.

53. See the section in chapter three on "emergent meaning" for further discussion of this idea.

mance. The very outline of *Holy Things* reveals this balance. The first section traces foundational patterns of Christian liturgy, relying largely on historical texts to show how the ordo emerged over time and achieved ecumenical usage. Then, in the second section of the book, he turns to the "things" of liturgical practice, going to the place of worship and asking "what the assembly actually says about God" in performance.[54] Moreover, he acknowledges the irony of what he is doing: creating a text to describe the practice even as he is calling for closer attention to the practice itself rather than the text. Therefore, he says, "We will reflect on these things and their interactions, here on the page. But now, especially, the reflections must be seen as an invitation to participate at the place of primary liturgical theology, to go into a church."[55] Understand that this text, even this ritually sensitive text, is secondary. The practice is primary.

One example of Lathrop's attention to local practice follows his question "What do you need to have church?" He answers that you need some "things."

> These can be as simple as the small breadroll, the little bottle of wine, the Sierra cup, and the pocket Bible pulled from a pack and spread on a bandana on a rock beside a rushing stream so that the backpacking group might gather as a church. Or they may be as magnificent as the golden chalice and paten, the jeweled book, the jeweled cross, and the flowing fountain that the sixth-century apse mosaics of San Vitale in Ravenna show the imperial couple, Justinian and Theodora, and their courtiers presenting as endowment to the local church. Essentially, the backpackers and the Byzantine court are bringing the same things.[56]

The contrast of these examples shows that all liturgies use specific concrete objects, even as those different objects have some basic similarities.

Lathrop and Collins are two prominent examples of contemporary liturgical theologians who have both diagnosed and responded to the

54. Lathrop, *Holy Things*, p. 87.
55. Lathrop, *Holy Things*, p. 87.
56. Lathrop, *Holy Things*, p. 88.

problem of textual preoccupation that characterized an earlier generation of liturgical scholars. In their work, they have shifted the focus to
texts *in practice,* actual liturgical performances as the site of primary
theology.

While a narrow focus on texts characterized an earlier generation of
liturgical theologians, contemporary scholars are largely aware of this
problem and are trying in various ways to respond to it with a new interest in liturgy as practice. This, however, has led to another problem
among some theologians: the tendency to use structuralist principles
in a way that obscures real differences in practice. As noted above,
Jennings in his 1987 article cited the structuralist approach as one
promising tool that ritual studies might offer to liturgical theology. He
says there, "This structuralist analysis provides tools for the analysis of
complex systems of signifiers into the reciprocal and oppositional relationships which govern them and constitute them as a structure. The
judicious use of such a methodology helps to display the 'depth grammar' that governs the apparent anarchic profusion of meanings at the
surface of such a structure."[57] Clearly, the benefit of such a form of
analysis is that it accounts for differences while insisting that there is a
common foundation beneath the "surface." Structuralism accords well
with the interest in basic liturgical shape that has characterized liturgical theology at least since Gregory Dix.[58] Therefore, several scholars, including Kavanagh, Fagerberg, and Lathrop, have employed structuralist theory in their liturgical theologies.[59]

Kavanagh endorses the use of structuralism in liturgical studies to
overcome the tendency to deal with liturgy as an abstraction. He
points out that talking about "liturgy" as if it were one undifferentiated thing obscures differences and can lead to unfounded generalizations. To prevent this from happening, he suggests a structuralist approach. This means living within a liturgical system for a period of
time, learning new vocabulary, alien grammar, different syntax in
both language and liturgy in order to experience the liturgical system
from the inside. Only after long effort will one then begin to move

57. Jennings, "Ritual Studies and Liturgical Theology," p. 44.
58. See Gregory Dix, *The Shape of the Liturgy* (Westminster: Dacre, 1945).
59. See for example Lathrop, *Holy Things,* pp. 33f. and *Holy People,* pp. 106f., in addition to the following references to Kavanagh and Fagerberg.

from this surface to the deep structure of the liturgical system. And it is at this deep level that commonality is to be found among the variety of liturgical practices.[60]

This use of structuralism has the apparent benefit of focusing on actual liturgical structures rather than inventing something called "liturgy" out of a set of unexamined assumptions.[61] Furthermore, it insists on the objectivity of liturgical meaning; one can read meaning off of the structure rather than equating meaning with participants' idiosyncratic interpretations. But ironically, and despite Kavanagh's intention, searching for "deep structures" beneath the "surface differences" in liturgical practice can too easily dismiss apparent differences in practice as unimportant or see a particular liturgical example as so anomalous that it must be thrown out of consideration. Mary Collins criticizes structuralism on this account: "According to this theory, structural study of multiple performances of a given ritual or multiple versions of a given folktale or myth should disclose those which are 'correct' and expose the inadequacy of those which are 'incorrect' or distorted versions. . . . Its purpose is limited. It presumes to deal with the fundamental nature of human cognition and communication, and has little interest in the communicated or perceived meanings themselves."[62] Although Kavanagh sees structuralism as a way to honor difference while affirming similarity, Collins points out that in its search for commonality, this approach can actually create a new abstraction which is judged to be purer than any specific example of it.[63]

A structuralist approach used by itself leaves little room for particularity and subjectivity in liturgical practice. Variations from the norm tend to be treated as annoying anomalies rather than genuine sources

---

60. See Kavanagh, *On Liturgical Theology,* pp. 79-80. Cf. pp. 129-30. Kavanagh in this discussion makes use of an article by Robert Taft, "The Structural Analysis of Liturgical Units: An Essay in Methodology," *Worship* 52, no. 4 (July 1978): 314-29.

61. This is Kavanagh's point, also made by Fagerberg, *What Is Liturgical Theology?* pp. 17, 180.

62. Mary Collins, "Ritual Symbols and the Ritual Process," pp. 63-64.

63. This critique is related to Catherine Bell's critique of some ritual theory: reification and romanticism of "liturgy" runs some of the same risks as reification and romanticism of "ritual." All liturgy, like all ritual, is particular. All liturgy, like all politics, is local. See Bell, *Ritual: Perspectives and Dimensions* (New York: Oxford University Press, 1997), pp. 253-67.

of meaning.[64] Collins points out that the understanding of *lex orandi* among liturgical theologians has been so influenced by structuralism that it has become excessively objective and abstract. To address this concern, she proposes that a structuralist approach be used in conjunction with "situational analysis," an approach developed largely by Victor Turner. Unlike Lévi-Strauss, who was primarily interested in consistency, "Turner focuses on the idiosyncratic processes of choice and on the way in which persons deal selectively with options from among operative values, structures, and symbolic forms according to the requirements of a situation."[65] Turner, using situational analysis, is more interested in particular concrete rituals and liturgies rather than an underlying deep structure that unites all liturgies. Collins endorses Turner's methodology as a helpful corrective to structuralism: "By pursuing this broadened line of inquiry about choice, the liturgical theologian may advance toward an understanding of the faith expressed in liturgical celebration not as an abstract and universal datum but as a living reality culturally expressed and culture laden."[66] In other words, through an approach that considers concrete situations as well as underlying structures, one may modify the usual understanding of *lex orandi* so that it avoids universalizing tendencies and becomes genuinely local.

Liturgical Theology in a Tradition That "Worships"

Liturgical theologians offer a serious critique of the common understanding of worship in the Reformed tradition. Schmemann charges that worship is currently understood as "bestowal of spiritual experience" instead of the epiphany of the church's being.[67] In liturgy, the church is supposed to be most fully itself, revealing its nature to the world and thus acting as source of all theology. But over the centuries, liturgy has deteriorated to become "at best, 'inspiration' and, at worst,

64. See Collins, "Critical Questions for Liturgical Theology," pp. 116-17.

65. Collins, "Ritual Symbols and the Ritual Process," p. 65.

66. Collins, "Critical Questions for Liturgical Theology," p. 119. Jennings also suggests using both structuralist and "dramatistic" approaches to liturgical analysis in his article "Ritual Studies and Liturgical Theology," pp. 44-45.

67. Schmemann, *Introduction to Liturgical Theology,* p. 25.

a meaningless 'obligation' to be reduced, if possible, to a valid minimum."[68] Kavanagh points to the sixteenth century as the time when
the appreciation of liturgy as primary theology gave way to a new understanding of liturgy as a means to an end:

> A sense of rite and symbol in the West was breaking down and
> under siege. And since it now appears that those who sought to
> repair the breakdown were its products rather than its masters,
> they may be said with greater accuracy to have substituted some-
> thing in its place that was new and, to them, more relevant to the
> times. It was a new system of worship which would increasingly
> bear the burden formerly borne by richly ambiguous corporate
> actions done with water, oil, food, and the touch of human
> hands. . . . Liturgy had begun to become "worship." . . . And the
> primary theological act which the liturgical act had once been
> now began to be controlled increasingly by practitioners of sec-
> ondary theology whose concerns lay with correct doctrine in a
> highly polemical climate.[69]

These critiques are certainly ones that the Reformed tradition
needs to hear. We have too often regarded secondary theology as the
master of liturgy, or, as I have put it elsewhere, we have regarded liturgy as simply the acting out of prior doctrine. We have diminished
the material signs and exalted the disembodied word as that which
will save us. And yet it is also the case that even within the Reformed
tradition there have been theologians such as Calvin and Nevin who
have lifted up the deeply formative character of liturgy, who have
hinted at its role as *theologia prima*. Even in the Reformed tradition, so
enamored of texts and printed worship bulletins, there is a growing
appreciation for the material symbols that Calvin insisted were necessary for the faith. And even in the Reformed tradition, there is respect
for the ecumenical ordo that Lathrop outlines as the deep structure of
Christian liturgy.[70]

---

68. Schmemann, "Liturgy and Theology," p. 95.
69. Kavanagh, *On Liturgical Theology,* pp. 108-9. See also Fagerberg, *What Is Liturgical Theology?* pp. 11-12, 184ff.
70. This can be seen particularly in the development of the 1993 *Book of Common*

At this point in history, we need to recover the understanding, from inside and outside the Reformed tradition, that liturgy is both anthropological rite and an occasion for divine self-manifestation. In order to do this, we need to look at specific liturgical events in a community, asking what sort of theology is emerging here, what relationships are being formed, what concrete actions are, over time, doing to the gathered people. In order to help in that task, we turn next to contemporary ritual theory, to gather some tools for understanding what it means to claim that liturgy, that the eucharist, is a *ritual*. As we will see, this lens for reading the eucharist focuses particularly on ritual as *doing*. *Lex orandi,* ritual theorists remind us, is *lex agendi.*

Worship, which presents as normative the balance of Word and Table each Lord's Day. This *Book* also emphasizes that texts are much more than printed words, but must be performed to be truly worship. Fred Holper discusses this explicitly in his address introducing the *Book of Common Worship,* "The Promise of Presbyterian Liturgical Renewal," in *Praying in Common,* Theology and Worship Occasional Paper no. 6 (Louisville: Presbyterian Church, USA, 1994), pp. 15-28.

CHAPTER 3

Lex Orandi *Is* Lex Agendi:
Resources from Ritual Theory

In chapter one, I argued that Calvin himself offers helpful theological resources to focus attention on the ritual dimension of the eucharist. Although some of his successors in the Reformed tradition have diminished the tangible, embodied aspect of the Lord's Supper in favor of explanation, Calvin's struggle for balance of Word and sacrament persisted in such theologians as John Williamson Nevin. In our current context, however, some Reformed Christians tend to concentrate on articulated doctrine as prior to holy encounter. This effectively transfers attention from the eucharistic action itself to theological explanation outside the liturgical sphere. We need to return attention to what happens in the eucharist as a site of divine action.

The exploration of themes in liturgical theology in chapter two provided some helpful models for approaching theology, and especially eucharistic theology, from the point of view of practice. Liturgy is primary theology, the *lex orandi* that shapes *lex credendi,* to use the familiar terminology.[1] Therefore we must begin with attention to real liturgies in living communities.

---

1. The term *lex agendi* has been helpfully suggested by Don Saliers to refer to the ethical pattern of intention and action fostered by the liturgy. See Saliers, *Worship as Theology: Foretaste of Glory Divine* [Nashville: Abingdon, 1994], p. 187; see also E. Byron Anderson and Bruce T. Morrill, eds., *Liturgy and the Moral Self: Humanity at Full Stretch Before God* (Collegeville, Minn.: Liturgical Press, 1998), pp. 6-8. Although my use of the term does have ethical implications, I intend *lex agendi* to point simply to the active, performative nature of liturgy itself. *Lex orandi* is about doing, about *agendi* — both ours and God's.

In this chapter, I lift up particular themes from contemporary ritual theory which correct both the disembodied approach to the eucharist propounded by some Reformed theologians and the preoccupation with abstract structures that has plagued much liturgical theology. These themes will, I hope, enable us to read the eucharist with new eyes, recovering Calvin's attention to the work of the Spirit in and through the sacrament. Through the lens of ritual theory, we will be able to see the *lex orandi* as first and foremost about doing, as a *lex agendi* in which participants are both engaged in embodied activity and also formed by patterns of liturgical action over time.

As a theologian, I recognize that I am embarking on dangerous territory here. By attending to rituals as rituals, by listening carefully to the work of scholars who make claims about what ritual activity does in and of itself, I could give the impression that the work of the Holy Spirit is incidental to the distinctively Christian practice of the eucharist. We will have to tread carefully in the pages ahead. What I offer in this chapter is not so much theology itself, but an exploration of recent findings in social scientific literature, findings that may prove useful when placed in conversation with theological discourse around the sacraments. In the process, I do not mean to reduce the Lord's Supper to simply another ritual, but I do intend to examine it as, among other things, an instance of human ritual activity.

A final disclaimer before beginning: as Catherine Bell points out, "'Ritual' is not an intrinsic, universal category or feature of human behavior," but is a historical construction that has meant different things to different people in different cultures.[2] I am not, therefore, attempting a transhistorical definition of ritual here, but am highlighting some claims made by recent ritual theorists who point to the active, embodied, and transformative aspects of rituals. By lifting up this profile of ritual activity, I am trying to redress the lopsided view of sacramental activity presented by many Reformed theologians.

---

2. Catherine Bell, *Ritual: Perspectives and Dimensions* (New York: Oxford University Press, 1997), p. ix.

Rituals *Do*

The first thing to point out is that rituals are about *doing*. This may seem obvious, but in fact for many modern Western people, the first question about a ritual is "What does it *mean?*" Edward Muir argues in his book *Ritual in Early Modern Europe* that in the sixteenth century, there was a major shift in understanding of rituals. According to the earlier view of the medieval Catholic church, rituals made something present; they did something. According to the newer view of the reformers, rituals communicated meaning; they meant something.[3] As a result, rituals were no longer conceived as presenting reality. They *re*presented a reality that existed elsewhere. The clearest example of this is the shift in eucharistic theology, from the medieval view that the eucharist literally presented the body of Christ to (in its most extreme form) the Zwinglian view that the eucharist represented the last supper Jesus shared with his disciples. The eucharistic meal no longer made present a reality; it pointed to a reality beyond itself. Its effectiveness thus required proper interpretation.[4] Muir blames this "hermeneutical assault on ritual" for the contemporary Western assumption that the point of rituals is their meaning.[5] He concludes that "the modern attitude perpetrates a misunderstanding that ritual must be interpreted, its hidden meanings ferreted out, when what rituals do is not so much mean as emote."[6] While Muir's assertion that "doing" equals "emoting" is rather reductionistic, his primary point is a helpful one: that rituals are about doing, not just meaning.[7]

3. Edward Muir, *Ritual in Early Modern Europe* (Cambridge: Cambridge University Press, 1997), pp. 7-8. This critique is related to Kavanagh's critique of the breakdown of rite and symbol in the sixteenth century; see *On Liturgical Theology*, pp. 108-9, also cited above in chapter two, note 69.

4. As we have already seen, and as Muir himself acknowledges, his characterization of the shift from doing to meaning does not adequately portray Calvin's eucharistic theology, since Calvin insisted that in the Lord's Supper, something really does happen: the Holy Spirit joins the faithful to Christ. Nevertheless, Muir's attention to the shift from what *happens* to what it *means* helpfully illumines the modern tendency to focus on the meaning rather than the doing of ritual.

5. Muir, *Ritual in Early Modern Europe*, p. 150.

6. Muir, *Ritual in Early Modern Europe*, p. 274.

7. Muir's easy assertion that what rituals do is emote goes directly against the view of many liturgical theologians, who insist that the reduction of liturgy to emotion is misleading. See, for instance, David Fagerberg's critique of Wainwright in *What Is Li-*

Muir's emphasis on ritual doing is shared by many contemporary theorists. David Parkin pointed out in 1992 that the preceding decade had witnessed the rise of the popular idea that rituals do not just express abstract ideas but do something.[8] This scholarly consensus was a reaction against the view that rituals are a "paralanguage," expressing more fundamentally real ideas. Scholars such as Lévi-Strauss, Edmund Leach, Clifford Geertz, and the early Victor Turner tended to describe rituals as expressing symbols or patterns, implying that those ideal symbols or patterns had a greater degree of reality than the empirical ritual activity. This approach has been called "symbolic," "semantic" or "semiotic" because of its focus on meaning.[9] By contrast, Parkin, Muir, and many others have shifted the focus to doing. Some have even contended that rituals have no intrinsic meaning at all, but are "meaningless."[10] In Christian ritual, I will suggest later, rituals both mean and do. However, for a theological tradition that has been preoccupied with meaning, there is a need to point out that rituals are also about doing.

Rituals are about doing in several senses. Most obviously, they are about physical doing: dancing, singing, eating, kneeling. Rituals involve actions. In another sense, rituals are about doing in that they affect the world of the participants: they create relationships, negotiate issues of identity and power, and order worldviews. Rituals relate and create. Finally, rituals are about doing in the sense of affecting the world as a whole: presenting models for a different world and even changing social structures. Rituals can transform. All of these aspects of doing are interrelated, but I will address each of them separately.

Rituals Involve Actions

Let us begin with the obvious. Roy Rappaport suggests in his essay "The Obvious Aspects of Ritual" that "in their eagerness to plumb rit-

---

turgical Theology? A Study in Methodology (Collegeville, Minn.: Liturgical Press, 1992), pp. 102-32. Even if Fagerberg is inaccurate in his assessment of Wainwright, his criticism that liturgy does more than create feelings can be directed to Muir.

8. David Parkin, "Ritual as Spatial Direction and Bodily Division," in *Understanding Rituals,* ed. Daniel de Coppet (London: Routledge, 1992), p. 14.

9. Bell, *Ritual: Perspectives and Dimensions,* pp. 62-68.

10. Frits Staal, "The Meaninglessness of Ritual," *Numen* 26, no. 1 (1975): 2-22.

ual's dark symbolic or functional depths, to find in ritual more than meets the eye, anthropologists have, perhaps increasingly, tended to overlook ritual's surface, that which does meet the eye."[11] What meets the eye in observing a ritual? Performance of that ritual involves persons doing particular things with their bodies in a particular physical environment. A ritual is not first and foremost about words. "Ritual is fundamentally made up of physical action," Parkin asserts; words are either absent or secondary. He goes on to claim, "I have never come across a ritual in which the spatial movements and orientation counted for nothing and the words were all-important."[12] So also Catherine Bell suggests in her book *Ritual: Perspectives and Dimensions* that the most important quality of ritual is the "primacy of the body moving about in a specially constructed space, simultaneously defining . . . and experiencing . . . the values ordering the environment."[13] The physical body moving in a particular environment is a central element, perhaps *the* central element, of ritual.

Take, for example, the ritual action of taking darśan at the Kali temple in Calcutta. I made the journey to Kalighat once in 1989 and twice in 1990, each time removing my shoes at the entrance and making my muddy way across the temple compound to the main pavilion which houses the image of the goddess Kali. Standing in the crowd before the closed doors of the shrine, I was aware of the mounting tension of those around me as we waited for the doors to open. Suddenly the bells began to ring, the doors were pulled open by the priests inside, and the crowd lunged forward, craning their necks to see the goddess. The central moment of that ritual, and the goal of every devotee there, was making direct eye contact with that black stone image and her blazing red eyes. The priests were reciting prayers, but clearly their words were not the focus of what was going on. That ritual has everything to do with the power of the gaze, and little to do with the hearing of the words.[14] Darśan in the Hindu tradition is all about what "meets the eye."

11. Roy A. Rappaport, "The Obvious Aspects of Ritual," in *Ecology, Meaning, and Religion* (Richmond, Calif.: North Atlantic Books, 1979), p. 174.

12. Parkin, "Ritual as Spatial Direction and Bodily Division," pp. 11-12, 17.

13. Bell, *Ritual: Perspectives and Dimensions*, p. 82.

14. For more on the phenomenon of darśan in Hindu worship, see Diana Eck, *Darśan: Seeing the Divine Image in India* (New York: Columbia University Press, 1998).

In the Christian worship tradition, rituals usually involve words as well as bodily actions. We do not stand wordlessly on tiptoe in the mud to catch a glimpse of a fire-eyed goddess. But our words are framed by particular embodied attitudes: we stand to sing (or not), we kneel to pray (or not), we walk in procession to receive a bit of bread and a sip of wine (or not). These embodied attitudes provide a significant context for the words we recite. Furthermore, the act of reading or repeating the words is itself a physical activity. Whether or not one is intellectually aware of the meaning of the text, participation in a corporate prayer or response involves the body. The same words of the Lord's Prayer may be sung joyfully to a Latin beat or mumbled in a monotone by a distracted congregation, in a Gothic cathedral or a half-finished mud-floored church in West Africa. The physical doing makes a difference.

The physical doing is critically important in the celebration of the eucharist. After all, since the earliest centuries, the movement of the Lord's Supper has been called the "fourfold action": take, bless, break, and give, based on Jesus' words of institution in 1 Corinthians 11.[15] The words are indispensable, but they are situated in the context of actions, and the recitation of the words is itself an action. So, in each celebration of the eucharist, the activity of physical bodies moving in a particular physical environment is a central element of the ritual.

As we have already heard from Calvin, human beings are made so that we need more than disembodied words. Calvin insisted on the unity of word and sacrament;[16] so also many ritual theorists insist that words cannot be divorced from their embodied performance. The words become flesh, so to speak, in particular physical environments and actions. This curious resonance between Calvin's theology and contemporary ritual theory is one we will explore more fully in the final chapter.

---

15. The importance of this "fourfold action" was retrieved by Dom Gregory Dix in his groundbreaking volume *The Shape of the Liturgy*. In the early centuries of the church, these actions developed into the offertory, eucharistic prayer, fraction, and distribution, which continues to be the common, though not universal, eucharistic pattern in churches around the world today.

16. Edward Muir even notes approvingly that "Calvin reoriented interpretation toward the material, visible bread, because without it there would be no sacrament, no mystical presence of Christ" (*Ritual in Early Modern Europe,* p. 175).

Rituals Affect and Effect Relationships

Another aspect of ritual doing has to do with the interaction between rituals and social relations. In brief, many recent ritual scholars have pointed out that ritual action can both modify existing relationships and create new relationships.

In one of the most intriguing essays on the effect of ritual on social relations, Roy Rappaport suggests that ritual "is *the* basic social act."[17] Rituals transmit two kinds of messages, according to Rappaport: "canonical messages," referring to processes or entities outside the ritual in words and acts that have been spoken before, and "indexical messages," referring to current physical, psychic, or social states of the participants.[18] In the act of performing a ritual, the performer becomes identical with the performance. As Rappaport says, "By performing a liturgical order the performer accepts, and indicates to himself [sic] and to others that he accepts, whatever is encoded in the canons of the liturgical order in which he is participating."[19] The acceptance of the canonical message by the performer is itself the indexical message of the ritual. This does not mean that the performer believes what he or she is performing, because private belief is not the same as public acceptance. It does not even mean that the performer will abide by the canonical messages of the ritual outside the context of the performance itself. But because the performance of ritual is a public act, it establishes the social conventions by which the community agrees to live. In other words, a man may participate in a liturgy that condemns adultery and still carry on an affair with his neighbor's wife, but the fact of his participation in the liturgy makes him morally accountable to the rule prohibiting adultery. Furthermore, ritual performances preserve the conventions of social order even when common usage violates them; the above example of adultery applies here as well. Even if adultery is widely practiced in a society, repetition of a liturgical order condemning the practice serves

17. Rappaport, "The Obvious Aspects of Ritual," p. 197.

18. This scheme closely resembles Tambiah's "semantic" and "indexical" meanings of ritual. See S. J. Tambiah, *A Performative Approach to Ritual,* Radcliffe-Brown Lecture 1979 (London: For the British Academy by Oxford University Press, 1981), pp. 153f.

19. Rappaport, "The Obvious Aspects of Ritual," p. 193.

to remind participants that the common practice is not the way things ought to be; the *is* stands in stark contrast to the *ought*. So, Rappaport concludes, "Ritual is unique in at once establishing conventions, that is to say enunciating and accepting them, and in insulating them from usage. In both enunciating conventions and insulating them, it contains within itself not simply a symbolic representation of social contract, but a consummation of social contract. As such, ritual . . . is *the* basic social act."[20] Rituals establish the social rules of a community, thereby ordering and governing all social relations. Without ritual, in this view, there would be no social organization at all.

This thesis makes a large claim for the power of ritual to establish the conditions for social relations. Rappaport is interested particularly in the way ritual preserves a given social order over time, even when the order is repeatedly violated by members of the community. Other ritual theorists have focused on the way rituals can alter existing social relationships. For example, Gerd Baumann argues that rituals do not simply display existing relationships; rituals also effect change in relationships. In particular, rituals can change the relationship between insiders and outsiders, between "us" and "them." As he puts it, rituals can be used to "convey a message across a cultural cleavage to 'others' or to an outside 'public' and . . . this message is concerned quite centrally with reformulating the cleavage between 'us' and 'them.'"[21] For example, in his analysis of Christmas celebrations among non-Christian Indian communities in London, he shows how "Others" (in this case, the majority Christian community) are implicated either "as physically present addressees or as absent categorical referents."[22] Through the appropriation and modification of the rituals of an English Christmas celebration, these communities negotiate their relationships with the dominant culture.

In his study of ritual wailing in the Warao culture of eastern Venezuela, Charles Briggs also notes this ability of rituals to change existing relationships. When a member of the community dies, Warao women

20. Rappaport, "The Obvious Aspects of Ritual," p. 197.

21. Gerd Baumann, "Ritual Implicates 'Others': Rereading Durkheim in a Plural Society," in *Understanding Rituals,* ed. Daniel de Coppet (London: Routledge, 1992), pp. 98ff.

22. Baumann, "Ritual Implicates 'Others,'" p. 99.

express personal and communal grief through ritual weeping. This is, Briggs points out, "the most important public performance genre accessible to women."[23] Through their words and music, Warao women borrow and rework the words used only by men in other public performance genres. In the process, they assign blame for each death in a way that produces real social consequences. For instance, when one young man in the Murako community dies, some of the wailers accuse four young men visiting from a nearby community of contributing to his death by making him an alcoholic. As a result, the four are escorted from the community and, "With one exception, they never returned to Murako."[24] In the course of another wailing, some women criticize the actions of a particular shaman, and he is subsequently ostracized by the community and forced to beg for food.[25] Briggs concludes from his study that "[i]n their laments, women . . . appropriate and use words initially used in settings where only men are accorded a voice. . . . In so doing, they question the dominant means of social (re)production and, in effect, act to constrain the authority of male shamans and political leaders."[26] While Briggs's research examines a particular ritual genre in a particular culture, he demonstrates that some rituals have the power to produce real change in social relations.

Briggs and Baumann point to a creative potential in rituals that can be observed also in Christian eucharistic celebrations. A moving example of this power is evident at the end of the controversial 1994 movie "Priest." In the film, a young English Catholic priest, Father Greg Pilkington, moves to a new parish and sets to work with great moral confidence trying to minister to the struggling urban congregation. He sharply criticizes his fellow priest in the parish, Matthew Thomas, an older man who has been carrying on a relationship with their housekeeper. In the confessional one day, Greg learns of a case of incest in his congregation. Torn between the desire to stop the suffering of Lisa, the girl involved, and his vow to maintain the confidentiality of the confessional, he resists informing Lisa's mother. Instead, he pleads with

23. Charles Briggs, " 'Since I Am a Woman, I Will Chastise My Relatives': Gender, Reported Speech, and the (Re)production of Social Relations in Warao Ritual Wailing," *American Ethnologist* 19 (1992): 338.

24. Briggs, " 'Since I Am a Woman,' " p. 337.

25. Briggs, " 'Since I Am a Woman,' " p. 347.

26. Briggs, " 'Since I Am a Woman,' " p. 337 (abstract).

Lisa to confront her father and to tell her mother of the situation. Lisa can do neither. Finally, however, the mother discovers the truth of what has been going on, and she turns on Father Greg for not telling her. In the midst of this trauma, the movie reveals that Greg is gay, and not the celibate cleric that he appeared to be when he harshly denounced Matthew. At the end of the movie, the congregation has been torn apart by the revelation of Greg's sexuality, the family has been torn apart by the revelation of sexual abuse, and Greg himself is torn apart by his own admission of moral hypocrisy and guilt. The last scene shows the two priests serving eucharist together to the congregation. When the invitation is issued for the people to come forward to receive the bread and wine, one by one the people rise and form a line in front of Father Matthew. No one comes to receive from Father Greg. Pale and trembling he stands at the head of the aisle, holding bread and cup, and no one will approach him. But just as he is about to give up hope, one person stands and slowly makes her way down the aisle toward him. It is Lisa, the young woman who was abused by her father. She hesitates, then comes and stands before the young priest and opens her mouth to receive the bread. She who needed healing and he who needed so much forgiveness come together in the eucharist. Surely this is an embodied act of forgiveness, the forging of a new relationship through a concrete ritual act. This is not the acting out of a reality that existed before; it is the reality itself, the emergence of a right relationship out of enormous pain.

Of course, this scene also shows how the ritual fails to transform the relationships of the majority of the congregation; most of the communicants approach Father Matthew and serve as foils for the new relationship revealed in Lisa and Father Greg. Even so, this simply demonstrates that the eucharist has the *potential* to alter relationships, not that it does so in an automatic way. In fact, at this point we may venture a theological interpretation of the scene: the action of the Holy Spirit is what gives the eucharist its power to transform the relationship between Lisa and Father Greg. The ritual itself does not determine the outcome in a mechanical way, but the eucharistic event provides a powerful medium through which the Spirit does its work of creation and re-creation. The medieval nominalist argument, so similar to Calvin's own, is relevant again here: if we believe that God can do anything according to absolute power, then we must observe to see what God is in fact doing according to God's ordained power.[27] If God works in and through the eucharist, this does not mean that divine action will work the same way every time; it means that we need to pay attention to see how God may be working in this particular instance.

Back to ritual theory. Rituals both transform existing relationships and forge new ones among people. A more daring assertion by ritual theorists such as Catherine Bell is that rituals not only construct relationships among persons, but that they create relationships between human beings and some external, often transcendent authority. As Bell puts it, "Ritualization tends to promote the authority of forces deemed to derive from beyond the present situation."[28] Through rituals, communities establish relationships with a "transcendent" or "divine" realm, outside the immediate material realm we can observe. Participants tend to see rituals as responding to or transmitting a reality, but, Bell argues, those rituals actually create the reality of human-divine relationships. We will discuss the theological implications of this assertion at greater length in the final chapter, but here I simply note that this view privileges the creative power of ritual, its role in establishing relationships not only between people, but between the human and the transcendent realm.

This emphasis on the power of rituals to establish and modify relationships can be set in fruitful conversation with Calvin's claim that the Holy Spirit operates through the eucharist to bind together the community of faith as the body of Christ. These are, obviously, different sorts of claims: to say that ritual does something in and of itself is not the same thing as saying that the Holy Spirit works in and through a ritual action to do something. Even so, in both cases, there is attention to a ritual/liturgical event as the site for creation and transformation of relationships. As I noted in the first chapter, Calvin's eucharistic interest is social rather than metaphysical; he is concerned about the community of believers being "engrafted into" the body of Christ. While Calvin's assertion focuses on the eucharist in particular, not rituals in general, ritual scholars' claims cohere in an interesting way with Calvin at this point: through the ritual performances of a community, relationships can be formed and transformed.

27. See chapter one, note 74.
28. Bell, *Ritual: Perspectives and Dimensions*, p. 82.

Rituals Create Meaning

Closely related to the idea that rituals create relationships is the view that rituals create meaning. Many ritual scholars, influenced by performance theory, have noted that rituals have an "emergent" quality, that is, they shift and adapt themselves to particular circumstances.[29] Charles Briggs, for instance, lists as a key aspect of performance its "emergence," which he defines as "the way structure and content are shaped by specific context."[30] Ritual performances are not pure reflections of some set "text," but are fluid events in which text and context interact creatively to produce new meaning. Similarly, Victor Turner noted in one of his last works that novelty and creativity "emerge" in the performance situation.[31] Only in performance does a ritual assume and project a particular meaning; this meaning cannot entirely be predicted beforehand.

By asserting that rituals create meaning, I am not reintroducing the position criticized earlier: that rituals *mean* rather than *do*. To say that rituals create meaning is not the same as saying that rituals only mean. The position that Edward Muir and others criticize suggests that rituals must be interpreted to discern the meaning they point to. The meaning is the true reality; the ritual simply points to it. Ritual action is, in effect, relegated to secondary status, while the "meaning" is of primary importance. On the other hand, the contention that rituals create meaning privileges the creative power of ritual action. This perspective focuses attention on particular performances, insisting that it is through concrete ritual actions that meaning comes into being. As Catherine Bell puts it in her summary of performance theory, "Ritual does what it does by virtue of its dynamic, diachronic, and physical characteristics, in contrast to those interpretations that cast ritual per-

29. For one of the earliest uses of this term, see Richard Bauman, *Verbal Art as Performance* (Prospect Heights, Ill.: Waveland Press, 1977), pp. 37ff. Stanley Tambiah also notes this quality of ritual, saying that emergent meanings depend on "existing grids of symbolic and indexical meanings, while also displaying new resonances" (*A Performative Approach to Ritual,* p. 160).

30. Charles Briggs, *Competence in Performance: The Creativity of Tradition in Mexicano Verbal Art* (Philadelphia: University of Pennsylvania Press, 1988), pp. 8ff.

31. Victor Turner, "The Anthropology of Performance," in *The Anthropology of Performance* (New York: Performing Arts Journal Publications, 1988), p. 76.

formances as the secondary realization or acting out of synchronic structures, tradition, or cognitive maps."[32] Far from downplaying the reality of ritual doing, this position holds that it is through doing that meaning is created. Meaning possesses no independent reality.

Furthermore, "meaning" here is not restricted to classic interpretations of a particular ritual. For example, the meaning of a communion meal is not only the recollection of Jesus' last supper, or the representation of Jesus' body within the community of faith, or even the engrafting of the faithful into the body of Christ. It may be all of these things, but it is also more. The meanings that are created by any given performance of communion include the mood of the gathered people, issues of their identity and power, as well as organization of their worldviews.

An example of this more expansive understanding of meaning is evident in Gloria Raheja's research on women's songs in North India. Raheja reports on the commonly held view that women are loved and respected in their natal homes, while they are less well treated in their married homes. These two sets of expectations are summed up in their roles as "sisters" and "wives." Sisters and wives are often regarded as being in conflict — and yet most women are both sisters and wives, producing a split identity. Some women's songs in North India reveal this conflict. If these songs were analyzed apart from performance, they would reveal a deep chasm between sisters and wives in a given family. But in the actual performance of these songs, a group of women gathers together to sing — often including both sisters and wives from the same extended family. This communal voicing of the tension between their roles provides a site of resistance to the split nature of their identities, since all women present are both sisters and wives and can understand and give voice to both perspectives. In this

---

32. Bell, *Ritual: Perspectives and Dimensions*, p. 75. Gloria Goodwin Raheja and Ann Grodzins Gold also present this view of the creative power of rituals in their "discourse-centered approach" to language and culture. They describe culture not as a set of structural fixities, but in terms of processes through which relationships are constructed, negotiated, and contested. Therefore, ritual performances do not only point to fixed meanings in the culture, but they actually shape those meanings in the process of performance. See Raheja and Gold, "Introduction," in *Listen to the Heron's Words: Reimagining Gender and Kinship in North India* (Berkeley: University of California Press, 1994).

way, performance creates a bridge both *among* women usually portrayed as hostile and *within* each woman, between her roles as sister and as wife.[33] This is the emergent meaning which can only be seen in concrete performance. The women's songs not only express hostility, they also forge relationships even in the midst of tension.

To be sure, meaning also precedes any given ritual performance. If there is any tradition or any intentional planning of a ritual, the performers and audience share a certain understanding of the ritual's purpose beforehand.[34] However, to emphasize the emergent quality of ritual is to recognize that even in the most carefully planned ritual, the details of performance cannot be controlled and the spirit of the gathering cannot be manipulated.

This emergent quality of ritual performance can best be grasped if one participates in or observes several performances of a given ritual over time. With some appreciation for the ongoing ritual patterns, one can better recognize the emergence of new interpretations in a particular situation. For example, in the previous chapter I described the shift in communion practice that occurred in one Presbyterian congregation as a result of worshiping in a Roman Catholic sanctuary. Accustomed to sitting in the pews to receive the elements, the congregation was suddenly faced with worshiping in a new context, which precipitated a change in practice: going forward to participate in communion. And as a result of this shift in practice, the eucharist became joyful feast more than sober individual reflection. Such a dramatic shift in mood was a direct result of the change in context, which produced a change in ritual action.

Meaning emerges in the actual performance of rituals. Again, this observation of ritual scholars may be set in fruitful conversation with Calvin's pneumatology as presented in the first chapter. As Calvin ar-

33. Gloria Goodwin Raheja, "On the Uses of Irony and Ambiguity: Shifting Perspectives on Patriliny and Women's Ties to Natal Kin" and "On the Uses of Subversion: Redefining Conjugality," in *Listen to the Heron's Words*, pp. 148ff.

34. Don Handelman emphasizes the priority of intentionality and design in rituals in *Models and Mirrors: Toward an Anthropology of Public Events* (Cambridge: Cambridge University Press, 1990), pp. 18, 20-21. I share Handelman's conviction that ritual events include both intentionality and performance, but here I am emphasizing what I think has been neglected by this interpretive tradition: the emergent quality of performance.

gues, the Holy Spirit moves within the community of faith to make Christ present through the sacrament. Therefore, we need to attend to the embodied performance of the eucharistic ritual to perceive how it is that God may be present in any given celebration. Though the work of the Holy Spirit is not simply identical with the principle of emergence, the theological discourse and the social scientific discourse are playing on a similar theme here. We are not entirely in control of the ritual, both the ritual theorists and Calvin remind us. Ranges of symbolic meaning are actually emerging in the context of the ritual performance. If we do not pay attention to the particularities of performance, we may miss it.

Rituals Transform

Entire social structures can be changed by rituals. This view stands in opposition to the description of ritual as merely perpetuating the status quo. David Kertzer, examining political rituals, notes that rituals tend to be more conservative than other aspects of culture, since part of their function is to link people with the past. Yet, "Paradoxically, it is the very conservatism of ritual forms that can make ritual a potent force in political change."[35] A frightening example of this ritual power is Hitler's use of ritual in his Nuremberg rallies to incite nationalistic fervor and loyalty to Nazism. Mohandas Gandhi used ritual power to bring about positive social change in India through the great salt march of 1930, in which people marched to the sea to make their own salt rather than paying the taxes imposed by the government. Likewise Martin Luther King, Jr., relied on ritual actions — the Selma march and spirituals such as "We Shall Overcome" — to give power to the civil rights struggle in the 1960s. In all of these cases, rituals were at least partly responsible for social transformation. As Tom Driver says, one of the most important gifts that rituals make to social life is "to assist the dynamic of social change through ritual processes of transformation."[36]

35. David I. Kertzer, *Ritual, Politics, and Power* (New Haven: Yale University Press, 1988), p. 12.
36. Tom F. Driver, *Liberating Rites: Understanding the Transformative Power of Ritual* (Boulder: Westview Press, 1998), p. 166.

It is important here neither to romanticize ritual nor to overestimate its power. As the Hitler example makes clear, rituals can bring about demonic social change. And, as any lifeless eucharistic celebration will demonstrate, rituals can also be simply ineffective. Stanley Tambiah provides a helpful set of terms that acknowledges both the transformative potential of ritual and its opposite tendency to drift into "empty ritual." As he puts it, rituals in history tend to oscillate between "poles of ossification and revivalism."[37] During periods of ossification, rituals tend to lose their semantic meanings, according to Tambiah. Deep societal rituals lose their cosmological significance and refer primarily to the social positions and power of the actors. In periods of revivalism, by contrast, semantic meanings of the rituals are paramount, while the "pragmatic," or political, meanings are less important. While I disagree with his contention that the rise of "pragmatic" meanings is directly related to ritual ossification, the ossification/revivalism polarity is nevertheless a helpful one. It reminds us that rituals are not always transformative.

Even so, many scholars concur that rituals can have a profound effect on social structures. One of the earliest ritual scholars to suggest this was Victor Turner, who contended that society operates with a dialectic of structure and "anti-structure" or *"communitas."* Structure is "society as a structured, differentiated, often hierarchical system of politico-legal-economic positions . . . separating [persons] in terms of 'more' or 'less.'" *Communitas,* on the other hand, refers to society as an unstructured community of equals, based on the "generic human bond without which there could be no society."[38] Both of these aspects are necessary for the healthy functioning of society. Turner argues that *communitas* emerges in the "liminal" state of rituals, a period of time when an individual or group is temporarily outside of the normal structures of life, with ambiguous social status. So rituals provide a release from normal hierarchical structures of society, a release which enables that society to continue to function. Turner himself observed in *The Ritual Process* that the rituals he was describing tended to reinforce the social structures. However, later in life he came to see rituals as "part of

---

37. Tambiah, *A Performative Approach to Ritual,* p. 165.
38. Victor Turner, *The Ritual Process: Structure and Anti-Structure* (New York: Aldine de Gruyter, 1995), pp. 96, 97.

the ongoing process by which the community was continually redefining and renewing itself."[39] Rather than returning the community to the same set of social relations that they had before, each ritual contributed to the redefinition of those relations. The *communitas* that emerges in the context of ritual performances, according to Turner, can indeed challenge and even transform the old hierarchical order.

Clifford Geertz was another early theorist to suggest that rituals have the potential for social transformation. He argued that rituals are both "models *of*" the way things are and "models *for*" the way things ought to be. So rituals both reflect and reshape the world around them.[40] It is the category of "model for" that points to rituals' ability to transform the world of the participants.

Don Handelman, a contemporary scholar who has further developed Geertz's terminology, also suggests that rituals may challenge the existing social order. However, rather than adopting Geertz's description of the two functions of rituals, Handelman describes three types of public rituals. In his work *Models and Mirrors,* he distinguishes among "events that mirror" (roughly equivalent to Geertz's "model of"), "events that model," and "events that re-present." Events that model intend to change the world, but they do so in specific, structured ways. It is the last category, events that re-present, that provides the opportunity for real social transformation. According to Handelman, events that re-present bring forward the underside of relationships and community, revealing what is normally concealed and concealing the usual social norms. Such a ritual can raise questions or doubts about the lived-in social forms. In such events, inversion is often used. This serves to reinforce social order — *unless* the inversion breaks its connection with what it inverts. If this happens, inversion threatens the old social order because it no longer rests on that order as a foundation.[41]

An example of this sort of ritual inversion threatening the social order is the contemporary celebration of Holi in northern India. Holi has long been celebrated as a spring festival in which the normal so-

39. Bell, *Ritual: Perspectives and Dimensions,* p. 39.

40. Bell, *Ritual: Perspectives and Dimensions,* p. 66. Also Clifford Geertz, "Religion as a Cultural System," in *Interpretation of Cultures* (New York: Basic Books, 1973), pp. 87-125.

41. Handelman, *Models and Mirrors,* pp. 49ff.

cial hierarchy is overturned. Low-caste people make fun of high-caste people by throwing colored water or powder on them, thus temporarily masking the observable differences among castes. It is a time of high spirits and practical joking, and in Victor Turner's terms, it releases the spirit of *communitas* without which there can be no functioning social order. Traditionally, the old social order resumes after the one-day festival.[42] However, in recent years the celebration of Holi has taken a more threatening, even violent turn in some communities. Young men, dissatisfied with their social positions, have begun throwing paint instead of water or powder, resulting in a more long-lasting "masking" of their victims. Physical attacks have taken place in some areas, as an escalation of the social chaos usually associated with this day.[43] In some places, Holi celebrations have even resulted in the physical injury or death of some participants. Clearly in these cases, the ritual inversion of Holi has broken its connection with the old social order, and real individual and communal suffering is the result. Yet despite the tragedies that accompany contemporary Holi celebrations, we can also see the violence as an attempt to redress the social injustices experienced by low-caste persons in Indian society. Attacks on individuals are also attacks on the system itself, and in humiliating or even killing their victims, the perpetrators are forcibly attempting to change the social structures. The license provided by the ritual of Holi transforms the social structure in a real, if violent, way.

The earliest Christians understood the eucharist in a similar way: as a ritual action that threatened the existing social order.[44] At table,

42. Or after the sixteen days of the festival, as celebrated in Vrindavan and Mathura. In these regions of India, Holi lasts much longer, but has the same function of overturning social hierarchy.

43. In a series of interviews with Indian film stars in 1999, this shift in Holi celebrations produced the following comments: "I used to celebrate it as a child, when we used to throw water balloons at each other. Now I feel it's a rough festival, and not my kind of festival" (Shilpa Shetty). "I think nowadays the real spirit of Holi has been lost and many youngsters use it to come closer sexually" (Bobby Deol). "Of late, it has taken an ugly turn. People use colors which don't come off for months together. Many colors are made of bad chemicals which are harmful for the skin and make it itch. Last year I had a lot of problems because I couldn't remove the colors from my hair for two to three months!" (Madhu).

44. For discussion of Jesus' meal practices as subverting the social order, see the writings of John Dominic Crossan and Marcus Borg, especially John Dominic Crossan,

Jesus broke bread and ate with sinners and outcasts. In the simple act of sharing meals, he reached beyond the boundaries that kept classes from each other. Herbert Anderson and Edward Foley, in their book on ritual and pastoral care, have even argued that "they killed him because of the way he ate; that is, because he ate and drank with sinners."[45] In the eucharist, the early church continued this dangerous practice, if not always easily, as we see in Paul's first letter to the Corinthians. Rich and poor sat down together, and thus the existing hierarchy was challenged by the enactment of community. While no one can argue that the celebration of the eucharist eliminated hierarchy in the Roman Empire, or even within the church itself in the long term, the ritual practices of Jesus and the early church certainly threatened the social structure of their day, presenting what Turner might call an example of *communitas,* or what Geertz might term a "model for" the way things ought to be. The eucharistic meal attempted to transform the social status quo by emphasizing the common humanity of all the table guests. This intention has been carried by the practice over time. Even when participants are not aware of it and even when structures are not immediately affected, the eucharistic practice bears within itself the challenge to social hierarchy, a challenge that has periodically been realized by Christian communities throughout history.

Does Calvin hint at the socially transformative power of the eucharist in his theology? He is ambivalent on this point, on the one hand maintaining strong boundaries around the table, but on the other hand emphasizing the ability of the Holy Spirit to bind together participants in the eucharist regardless of their social status. This much at least can be said: that Calvin recognized a connection between liturgy and ethics, between the act of the eucharist and the life of the Christian community in the world. If he was not primarily concerned with the transformation of unjust social structures, he was concerned with the role of this ritual in forming communities of love and faithfulness.

The Historical Jesus: The Life of a Mediterranean Jewish Peasant (San Francisco: Harper-SanFrancisco, 1991), and Marcus J. Borg, *Meeting Jesus Again for the First Time: The Historical Jesus and the Heart of Contemporary Faith* (San Francisco: HarperSanFrancisco, 1994), pp. 55-57. Crossan coined the term "open commensality" to describe Jesus' practice of eating with all, including sinners and tax collectors.

45. Herbert Anderson and Edward Foley, *Mighty Stories, Dangerous Rituals: Weaving Together the Human and the Divine* (San Francisco: Jossey-Bass Publishers, 1998), p. 155.

Conclusion

In this chapter I have tried to identify certain themes from ritual scholars that cast a new light on theological reflection on the Lord's Supper. In particular, by lifting up "doing" as primary in rituals, I am trying to counterbalance the emphasis on theological explanation that has characterized (or caricatured?) much Reformed sacramental theology since Calvin. Performative power is not exhausted in any account of what a ritual "means." But in focusing on doing, it is important not to lose sight of the other side of the balance. To paraphrase Catherine Bell in her description of practice theory, rituals both do *and* mean. They both reproduce *and* transform past patterns. Individual participants both reproduce *and* transform their own predicaments.[46] Of course rituals can be conservative; they do not always redefine the world or eliminate social injustices, much as we might wish it to be so. But the point is that they can have a creative power. They do not merely reflect or re-assert a pre-existing reality. Rituals, including the eucharist, have a reality of their own. In focusing on ritual doing, I am trying to return attention to what actually happens in the ritual moment of the eucharistic celebration: the physical eating and drinking, the establishment or renewing of relationships, the emergence of new meaning, and even the transformation of the world. As we move from a consideration of social scientific literature into the realm of theological reflection, the tricky question becomes: How do we understand the relationship between the power of human ritual action in and of itself, as explored here, and the power of the Holy Spirit moving in and through the Christian performance of the eucharist?

---

46. See Bell, *Ritual: Perspectives and Dimensions*, p. 83.

CHAPTER 4

In Search of a Local Lex Orandi

In chapter one, I explored themes from the Reformed tradition that direct attention to the eucharist as a locus for God's presence and activity. I argued that, although the larger Reformed tradition is not unanimous, there is a persistent conviction that God does act in and through our communion practices. In communion, the Holy Spirit unites us with Christ and with each other as a result of divine freedom, and because of human need for the visible and tangible as well as audible. These claims are made by Calvin himself, as well as later Reformed theologians such as John Williamson Nevin.

In chapter two, I continued to explore the assertion that God works in and through the eucharist by drawing from contemporary liturgical theology. Even more strongly than most Reformed theologians, liturgical theologians insist that our knowledge of God comes primarily through the liturgy, which consists of both Word and sacrament. The Word proclaimed and the sacraments celebrated in the assembly mutually inform one another, so that (to borrow Calvin's language) the Word is audible sacrament and the sacrament is visible Word. The sacrament of eucharist, as focal point of traditional Christian liturgies, serves as the site where God and humanity meet in a particularly profound way. We encounter God at table, and subsequent reflection on that encounter constitutes articulated theology. The liturgy is the foundation for doctrine. *Legem credendi lex statuat supplicandi.*

Both traditional Reformed theology and contemporary liturgical theology point toward the liturgy, including the eucharist, as a place of holy encounter with God. Both Reformed and liturgical theologians insist that we must take seriously what happens at the table, because in and through that activity God is at work. But this brings us to the weakness that has so far handicapped both Reformed and much liturgical theology: lavish reflection on the common shape and dynamism of the eucharist, but insufficient attention to actual local practices. This criticism of both theological traditions is particularly clear in light of recent trends in ritual studies. Scholars such as Catherine Bell and Charles Briggs have sharply criticized the tendency of an earlier generation of ritual scholars to treat "ritual" as a universal phenomenon that may unwittingly perpetuate the status quo of a given society. Bell and others insist that we must guard against broad generalizations about "ritual" and pay closer attention to particular practices and the way they reflect and shape their contexts. With this in mind, I argue that we must be cautious about claiming too quickly what the eucharist is and does in any particular congregation. We must not allow the universal predetermined "meaning" of the ritual to blind us to the "doing" of particular eucharistic rituals in our local churches.[1]

This brings us to the task at hand. Holding on to the traditional Reformed assertion of Christ's "spiritual real presence" in the eucharist as well as the liturgical theologians' formula *legem credendi lex statuat supplicandi,* I turn to one particular local congregation to see what is being done there in and through their eucharistic practices. I am taking seriously the contention that theology is grounded in liturgy and asking the question, "What theology is emerging here?" What is the local *lex orandi,* and how is it shaping this church's *lex credendi?*

This raises the question of what exactly is meant by a "local *lex orandi.*" I intend this to refer to the eucharistic practice of this congregation broadly considered; that is, the *lex orandi* includes 1) the event of worship itself: words, gestures, environment, and music here and now; 2) the history of worship in this congregation: how the liturgy

---

1. In one sense, even the theological assertion that the eucharist conveys God's grace is a normative claim that may not correspond to any given eucharistic celebration. Here we are in the thicket of descriptive-normative ambiguity: a simple descriptive statement about what the eucharist *is* presumes a normative ideal. Some ambiguity here is unavoidable, but in attending to particular local practices, I am trying to present the fine-grained descriptive task as a necessary correlate of the broad normative theological claim.

has formed participants in this place over time; 3) the individual interpretations that members bring to the celebration, both memories and
present experience; 4) the history of interpretation of this community,
which is itself shaped by the larger denominational and broadly ecumenical histories of interpretation; and 5) the tensions between new,
emerging practices and the preceding four elements.[2] Although I have
sought in earlier chapters to focus on the first element, the performed
event of liturgy, it is nevertheless critical to remember that liturgical
action does not exist in a vacuum. It is performed by, for, and through
persons who themselves have been shaped by varying histories of liturgical participation. As Calvin reminds us, without the faith of participants the eucharist is ineffective. Without human engagement, the
eucharist is not only empty; it is impossible. All of this is to say that
when we consider the *lex orandi* of any given community, we are considering a multifaceted and unavoidably social reality that shifts with
each new performance. *Lex orandi* is not a static monolith to which
the congregation comes; it is an ever-changing encounter of one community with each other, with the world, and with God.

In order to attend to the multidimensional nature of *lex orandi*, I
use a fourfold approach to analyze the local eucharistic practice of this
congregation. The four methods I employ to explore this local *lex
orandi* are: 1) phenomenological observation of eucharistic practice;
2) textual analysis of the liturgy; 3) individual and group interviews;
and 4) a survey distributed to a representative cross-section of the congregation. A word about each of these facets of my approach will be
helpful here:

Phenomenological observation. I use this term to refer to the careful
description of actual performances of the eucharistic ritual. Here, I am
particularly interested in the details of performance: What gestures did
the ministers use? Which words were emphasized, and which passed
over quickly? What did the congregation do during distribution of the
elements? How robustly did they sing? I am interested both in what
this congregation does in common with other Christian (and especially Presbyterian) congregations and in what ritual practices are
unique to this setting.

Textual analysis. In this step, I exegete the written texts of the

2. Don Saliers, private communication, July 24, 2000.

eucharist, both those used by the clergy and those available to the congregation. I analyze the theology evident in the texts themselves, and consider them in the wider historical context of earlier Roman Catholic, Orthodox, and, especially, Reformed eucharistic liturgies.

Although I am focusing attention on the embodied action of the eucharist, it is clear that to focus on the action without taking into account the experiences of the congregants themselves would be misleading. A substantial part of what the ritual action does is to form participants' affections and relationships, a facet of the ritual doing that cannot be seen by a detached observer. While Lathrop is helpful in contending that "primary liturgical theology is the communal meaning of the liturgy exercised by the gathering itself,"[3] and not the private act of individuals, the "communal meaning" includes the inner dynamics of the people in the pews. I therefore include two components in my study that focus on the congregation's experiences and interpretations, dimensions not visible to an observer of the ritual action as such:

Individual and group interviews. In this part of the project, I interviewed a cross-section of the congregation, selected with attention to representation of ages, gender, years of membership in this church, and levels of participation. The interviews focused on congregants' experiences of communion and ways in which those experiences are shaped by particular aspects of ritual. The rationale for conducting these interviews was twofold:

- to get a picture of the thoughts, feelings, expectations, and memories people bring to eucharistic celebrations, since these inner dynamics are part of the whole performance,[4] and
- to discern, as much as possible, how their understanding of eucharist is affected by concrete celebrations.

Congregational survey. This less nuanced instrument allowed me to get feedback from a greater number of congregational members, filling

3. Gordon Lathrop, *Holy Things: A Liturgical Theology* (Minneapolis: Fortress Press, 1993), p. 5.

4. Of course, such reported feelings and memories may be one-time perceptions, not necessarily representative of an interviewee's ongoing affective state. Nevertheless, taken as a group and with appropriate caution, such interviews can reveal something about the affections that are both formative of and formed by liturgical participation.

out the portrait of this congregation's eucharistic theology that I discerned from the observation, exegesis, and interviews. Like the interviews, the survey focused on the inner dynamics that people bring to eucharist as well as the ways these dynamics are affected by the outward celebration.[5]

What is the secondary theologian to do with this complex, multifaceted *lex orandi?* Having gathered and collated, listened and observed, read and reflected, the task is to interpret what is going on here. Like a detective, the theologian tries to piece together a coherent narrative out of the individual stories, the bits of food, the scraps of melody, the different cadences of pastoral leadership in this place. And gradually, from the pile of accumulated evidence, common themes begin to recur. Harmony begins to emerge out of the cacophony of voices. The theologian as interpreter of communal ritual can then present an account of what is going on in the community's primary theology — not in order to judge the practice from the standpoint of superior doctrine, but in order to enable fuller participation in that very practice. Articulated theology thus both begins and ends with *lex orandi.*

The structure of this chapter traces this process of description moving into interpretation. So in the first part of the chapter, I move diachronically through the structure of an ordinary communion service in this particular church, with examples drawn from the worship service described in the prologue. For each element of the liturgy, I include synchronic reflections on text and performance as well as related themes that emerged from interviews and surveys of the congregation. In the second part of the chapter, I lift up two major strands of eucharistic theology that co-exist in this church. Through this congregational study, I hope to illumine how competing primary theologies can be operative in a single community, and I will suggest that one of these strands of existing theology is more helpful in encouraging the full participation of persons in the eucharist.

5. For the text of the survey itself, see Appendix 1. For the full results of the survey, see Appendix 2.

Inviting: The Invitation to the Table

After preaching the sermon and praying a brief concluding prayer, the pastor ("Matthew") moves with the associate ("Mark") down the steps of the chancel to stand behind the communion table, which is on the floor of the sanctuary.[6] Matthew then addresses the congregation casually, without script, inviting all baptized believers to participate in communion. On this particular World Communion Sunday, he has preached on the "lunar communion service" celebrated by one church in Texas with Buzz Aldrin when he was on the surface of the moon. He picks up on that theme in the invitation: "This table . . . is a big table, welcoming not just Presbyterians, but all Christians, all believers, all baptized believers to partake of this meal — with brothers and sisters in Christ around this world and, at least one time, with a brother in Christ on the surface of the moon. It's a *big* table. And all baptized believers are welcome." His emphasis is on the expansiveness of the table, the breadth of the welcome issued here. The words make it clear that baptism is a precondition for participation in communion, but Matthew's delivery of the words downplays this aspect of the invitation in favor of a warm and direct welcome to come to the table.

This mention of baptism, the one theme that appears consistently in invitations to table in this church, is important for two reasons. First of all, it establishes a vital link between the two sacraments, baptism and communion. Baptism is the entrance into Christian life, as communion is the nourishment that sustains that life. Although mention of baptism is consistently part of the invitation to the table, it is remarkable that in the interviews, the only people who made a connection between the two sacraments were former Baptists, for whom participation in communion immediately followed their profession of faith and baptism. No lifelong Presbyterians (or members with roots in any other denomination) made this connection. Instead, most interviewees made a clear connection between communion and confirmation, which for generations replaced baptism as the rite of initiation into the Lord's Supper.

This brings us to the second reason that the mention of baptism in the invitation is important; namely, because it represents a change in

6. These are not the real names of the ministers.

church practice from an earlier generation. Until the 1970s, the official practice of mainline American Presbyterians was to invite children to the table only after they were confirmed.[7] One needed to reach the "age of discernment" before participating in communion. The underlying assumption was that it was important to understand what one was doing. This practice of admitting children to the table only after they reached the age of discernment began in the medieval era, when communion was restricted to the confirmed who had made a good confession of sin.[8] The practice continued with Calvin, who taught that although infants are to be baptized, they should not partake of communion until they reach an age to discern the body of Christ in the elements: "For with respect to baptism, the Lord there sets no definite age. But he does not similarly hold forth the Supper for all to partake of, but only for those who are capable of discerning the body and blood of the Lord, of examining their own conscience, of proclaiming the Lord's death, and of considering its power."[9] This is consistent with Calvin's interest in self-examination, as explored in the first chapter. It is necessary for the worshiper to have some capacity for discernment in order to participate rightly in communion. Within the context of Calvin's own eucharistic theology, this makes sense, since without some taste of faith, one cannot receive nourishment from the eucharist. As a church practice, however, it has often led to a problematic emphasis on intellectual capacity as a precondition for admission to table.

7. The age of confirmation itself shifted over the course of the twentieth century; whereas in the early decades of the century it was customary to confirm children at age 8 or 10, by the 1960s and 1970s, the age of confirmation was early to mid-teenage years. See "Admission to the Lord's Table," in *Selected Theological Statements of the Presbyterian Church (USA) General Assemblies (1956-1998)* (Louisville: Office of Theology and Worship of the PC [USA], 1998), p. 5.

8. The preponderance of infant baptism without confirmation in the West, which became common practice beginning in the fifth century, created this separation and delay. At the Fourth Lateran Council in 1215, it was mandated that confession should precede communion, officially enacting the connection between confirmation, confession of sin, and admittance to the table. See canon 21 of the Fourth Lateran Council, in Heinrich Denzinger, *Enchiridion Symbolorum: Definitionum et Declarationum de Rebus Fidei et Morum,* edition 31 (Freiburg: Herder, 1960), pp. 204f.

9. *Institutes* 4.16.30. This argument, and the ones that follow, are based on a reading of 1 Corinthians 11:28.

The Westminster Catechism, so influential in American Presbyterianism, echoed Calvin's teaching on this subject, focusing especially on the task of self-examination: "The Lord's Supper is to be administered often, in the elements of bread and wine . . . and that only to such as are of years and ability to examine themselves."[10] A quote from the 1921 *Book of Church Order* of the Presbyterian Church in the United States reveals that this continued to be the usual practice for most of the twentieth century:

> Children born within the pale of the visible church, and dedicated to God in baptism, are under the inspection and government of the church, and are to be taught to read and repeat the Catechism, the Apostle's [sic] Creed, and the Lord's Prayer. . . . And when they come to years of discretion, they ought to be urgently reminded that they are members of the church by birthright, and that it is their duty and privilege personally to accept Christ, confess him before men, and seek admission to the Lord's supper.[11]

Here, admission to the Lord's Supper is explicitly contingent upon confession of faith, given by those of "years of discretion."

This changed in the 1970s, when both branches of the Presbyterian Church specified that the only thing necessary to participate in communion was baptism, not confirmation.[12] The *Book of Order* now

10. Westminster Larger Catechism, question 177 in *Book of Confessions: Study Edition,* 7.287.

11. *Book of Church Order of the Presbyterian Church in the United States* (Richmond: Presbyterian Committee of Publication, [1921?]), pp. 150-51. Virtually the same text was included in the 1945 edition of the *Book of Church Order.*

12. In the UPCUSA (the northern Presbyterian church), there was a change in the Directory for Worship in 1971 to allow baptized children to come to the table, but this change in policy reflected a change in practice that was already in place in some congregations. See *Directory for Worship* in the *Book of Order* of the United Presbyterian Church in the United States of America (1971), chapter V, section 2, par. 10 (20.02); cf. 21.04 and 41.06. At least by the early 1970s, some in the PCUS (the southern church) adopted this practice, but it was not adopted by the General Assembly until 1976 and did not enter the Book of Church Order until 1980. See *Book of Church Order,* Presbyterian Church in the United States 1980/81 edition (Atlanta: Office of the Stated Clerk of the General Assembly, PCUS, 1980), Part II, chapter 7-3. At the reunion of the two de-

reads "Baptized children who are being nurtured and instructed in the significance of the invitation to the Table and the meaning of their response are invited to receive the Lord's Supper, recognizing that their understanding of participation will vary according to their maturity."[13] Thus the minister is clear when inviting people to the table that all baptized believers are welcome.

The earlier practice of barring children from the table until confirmation still lingers in the memories of most congregants, however, deeply affecting the way they experience communion. As a result, the link between baptism and eucharist, although explicitly proclaimed in the invitation, has been obscured, and admittance to the table has become a rite of passage into adulthood, a sign and seal that one understands the meaning of the mystery there. This view of communion feeds the general view I call "Lord's Supper as individual devotion" below, the attitude that values individual interpretation of meaning over outward practice.

This single liturgical element, the invitation to table, is a prime example of the complexity involved in theological interpretation. On the one hand, the **words** of the invitation provide a view of eucharist in which the meal unites the covenant community of believers joined by baptism. At the same time, the **performance** of these words downplays the implicit boundary imposed by the baptismal language in favor of a table that is open to all. And the **memory** at work in many participants operates in a third direction again: interpreting those invited to the table as those who have made a mature profession of faith. We can already see in this first movement of the eucharist that even when a liturgical act is apparently simple and straightforward, it can feed divergent eucharistic theologies.

---

nominations in 1983, the new *Book of Order* of the PC (USA) included the former UPCUSA statement advising the session to counsel parents who permitted baptized children to take communion. So, although it has been the norm in some churches for over thirty years, it is still a relatively new practice in many congregations, including this one.

13. Directory for Worship, *Book of Order* (Louisville: Presbyterian Church [USA], 2002-2003), W-2.4011b.

Thanking: The Great Prayer of Thanksgiving

Following the pastor's invitation to the table, the associate pastor proceeds with the Great Prayer of Thanksgiving. This begins with the *sursum corda,* the element so important to Calvin's eucharistic theology: "The Lord be with you / **And also with you.** / Lift up your hearts. / **We lift them up to the Lord** . . ." For Calvin, this response was critical to turn the people's attention from the earthly things to Christ in glory at the right hand of the Father.[14] He understood the *sursum corda* as a way to guard against idolatry of the material elements, the central problem he saw in the Roman Catholic doctrine of transubstantiation. Here at First Presbyterian, the *sursum corda* functions as a preparation for prayer. The congregation knows the dialogue more or less by heart, and so they recite the words while settling into an attitude of prayer: bowed heads, closed eyes, quiet bodies.

The eucharistic prayer proceeds according to an ancient pattern: opening preface addressed to God the Father, concluding with the Sanctus, then the middle section remembering Jesus Christ, concluding with the memorial acclamation, and the final epiclesis calling on the Holy Spirit to sanctify these gifts of bread and wine and make them be "for us" the body and blood of Christ. It concludes with the Lord's Prayer.[15] The Great Prayer varies in exact wording from one celebration of communion to another, but it is usually taken from the Presbyterian *Book of Common Worship,* the comprehensive worship resource for the denomination, published in 1993. On this particular

---

14. See above, chapter one, pp. 24-26, 31. See also John Calvin, "The Form of Church Prayers and Hymns with the Manner of Administering the Sacraments . . . ," in Bard Thompson, *Liturgies of the Western Church* (Cleveland: William Collins and World Publishing Co., 1961), "Form of Church Prayers," p. 207.

15. This pattern is similar to the basic form that was in place for eucharistic prayers by the end of the fourth century. According to Jasper and Cuming in *Prayers of the Eucharist,* the basic (West Syrian) form consisted of the following pattern: sursum corda, preface, pre-sanctus, sanctus, post-sanctus, institution narrative, anamnesis, offering, epiclesis, intercessions, and doxology. See R. C. D. Jasper and G. J. Cuming, eds., *Prayers of the Eucharist: Early and Reformed,* 3rd ed. (Collegeville, Minn.: Liturgical Press, 1990), p. 6. The eucharistic prayer at First Presbyterian does not include the institution narrative, which is placed after the prayer; also, the intercessions are located in a separate prayer earlier in the service. Otherwise, the form is the same.

day, the associate uses the Great Prayer of Thanksgiving C, with the proper preface designated for World Communion Sunday.[16]

The use of the traditional eucharistic prayer in this church came into practice with the current associate pastor, so the form is still new to many members of the congregation.[17] Still, they participate in the responses, both spoken and sung, robustly enough, and after two and a half years, some have even memorized the Sanctus setting that is used in every communion service. Although it is dangerous to infer too much from robust singing (it could, after all, be simply a case of enthusiastic music lovers who have absolutely no concern for textual content), the consistent and attentive participation of the congregation in the responses suggests some level of genuine engagement in the liturgy, some receptivity to the work of God in and through the assembly at prayer.

The formal style of the Great Prayer contrasts with the more conversational approach of the pastor's invitation, a contrast that is consistent with the overall style of these two ministers. The associate pastor, Mark, seeks to use the liturgical tradition in prayers and responses, while Matthew opts for a looser, often unscripted form of address. Ironically, this has produced a pattern over their ministry together in which Matthew speaks to the people and Mark speaks on behalf of the people to God. In the eucharistic service, this means that Matthew issues the invitation, Mark offers the Great Prayer, Matthew recites the Words of Institution from memory, they both distribute the elements, and Mark offers the closing prayer. In effect, Matthew directs his attention primarily to those within the walls of the sanctuary (a more "pastoral" function), while Mark directs the congregation's attention be-

16. See *Book of Common Worship* (Louisville: Westminster/John Knox Press, 1993), pp. 130-32, 133.

17. This despite the fact that the traditional eucharistic prayer form has been included in Presbyterian worship resources since at least 1946. The 1946 *Book of Common Worship* of the northern Presbyterian Church had a lengthy eucharistic prayer with sursum corda, proper prefaces, sanctus, anamnesis, and epiclesis. A similar form was published in the 1970 *Worshipbook*, developed by the Joint Committee on Worship for both the northern and the southern Presbyterians. The 1993 *Book of Common Worship* has several versions of the eucharistic prayer, but the form is hardly new to this denomination. Still, because the use of the denominational worship resources is not mandatory, but is left to the discretion of local pastors and sessions, the publication of the form in denominational resources has not brought about wide usage in congregations.

yond the walls, serving as the link between this local church, the church universal, and the triune God (a more "priestly" function).

From this description it might appear that Mark possesses the greater authority in the eucharistic service, standing in the classic role of priest interceding for the people before God. Yet this is not the case, for it is Matthew who subtly controls the tone and tempo of the liturgy, issuing the invitation, cuing Mark with a nod when it is time to pray, and at one communion service actually skipping over the eucharistic prayer altogether to move directly to the Words of Institution. This is a ministerial partnership that works smoothly most of the time, but the eucharistic service makes it clear that the balance of power is not absolutely equal.

How does this difference in styles of presiding, coupled with the difference in authority, affect the primary, performed theology of this community? Positively, the two voices help to balance each other, one focusing on the simplicity of the meal offered to this community, and the other situating the meal in the broad context of salvation history and the tradition of the wider church catholic. But because the two ministers do not operate with absolutely equal authority, the liturgical elements led by the more senior minister have slightly more emphasis in the whole communion service. As a result, there is a focus on *this* community and direct engagement of their attention, and a downplaying of attention to the ancient tradition. Further, as I will discuss in the following section on the Words of Institution, the division of labor between the ministers subtly focuses attention on the Words as the central act of communion, the liturgical element for which the Great Prayer is preparation. Those elements of the Great Prayer that are not directly connected with the Words and their echoing of the Last Supper thus have less prominence in the congregation's primary theology.

This can be illustrated by a quick analysis of the components of the eucharistic prayer and a comparison of these themes with the themes that frequently emerged in the interviews. The Great Prayer includes the following elements: thanks for God's creation of all things, and especially of these gifts; joining of this community's praise with the communion of saints; thanks for Jesus Christ's incarnation, ministry, death, resurrection, risen presence, and anticipated return; offering of ourselves; prayer for the Holy Spirit to sanctify these elements; connection of Christ's body and blood with this assembly as Christ's body

118

redeemed by his blood; prayer that the assembly may be sent out to proclaim Christ to the world; prayer for the unity of these people with Christ; and anticipation of the coming of Christ at the end of time. But only some of these themes appeared in the interviews with congregational members.

To be sure, the Great Prayer of Thanksgiving is first and foremost an opportunity to thank God for all good gifts, and especially for the gift of Jesus Christ. This attitude of thanksgiving ought to characterize all of our lives, according to Calvin; the eucharistic prayer is thus both illustrative of and formative of the gratitude that ought to be the basic stance of the human in relation to God.[18] And many congregational members articulated and experienced a connection between communion and gratitude. For them, celebration of the eucharist does indeed prompt a grateful response for God's goodness.

Some of those interviewed described thankfulness in personal terms, like the woman who defined the heart of communion as "giving up fears of what others think of you and accepting the love that is given every day." For some, participation in communion is linked to a profound sense of God's grace to them because of a conversion experience or "spiritual rebirth" earlier in life. One older man admitted that early on in life, he carried a lot of guilt and disappointment in himself, but gradually that changed, and therefore his experience of communion changed. Now he sees communion as a second chance, as a real experience of grace. "I typically end up in awe anymore of how that could be provided for me. I used to end up wondering why somebody like *me* would be given that." Others describe being thankful more generally for the gift of Jesus Christ: "this wonderful gift of grace," "such a gift of love," "such a precious gift of love." Only one interviewee specifically connected the prayer of thanksgiving with her sense of gratitude; she named the prayer of thanksgiving as the most important part of communion, "because you are acknowledging the gift." But even without explicit reference to the liturgical form, it is

---

18. As Brian Gerrish notes, "The holy banquet is simply the liturgical enactment of the theme of grace and gratitude that lies at the heart of Calvin's entire theology" (*Grace and Gratitude: The Eucharistic Theology of John Calvin* [Minneapolis: Fortress Press, 1993], p. 20). Though Gerrish does not link this theme with the prayer of thanksgiving in particular, this is the liturgical element that makes the theme of grace and gratitude most explicit.

clear that for many people in this congregation, the Lord's Supper is an occasion for gratitude for God's grace.

The frequent references to gratitude among those interviewed may be shaped by the fact that, even though the ancient pattern of the eucharistic prayer has not been long practiced in this setting, there is a long history of a "prayer of thanksgiving" as a part of communion services here, as was the general practice in twentieth-century American Presbyterianism. The content of that prayer would have varied according to occasion and presider, but it would certainly have focused on the gift of Jesus Christ, either presented by or represented by the bread and wine. The repetition of this liturgical element over many years, together with catechesis that congregational members received in Sunday school and classes preparing for communion — not to mention the theme of gratitude in preaching — have certainly contributed to this attitude of thankfulness associated with the eucharist.

But while this congregation does understand eucharist as an occasion for gratitude to God for all gifts, and especially the gift of Jesus Christ, there are many other themes in the Great Prayer that have little or no prominence in the congregation's lived experience. For instance, despite three references to the second coming of Christ in the Great Prayer — in addition to the one in the Words of Institution — there was no mention of the eschatological dimension in any of the interviews. Nor was there much attention paid to Christ's ministry before the Last Supper and crucifixion.[19] Most striking was the almost total lack of reference to the work of the Holy Spirit among those interviewed. In spite of the trinitarian shape of the Apostles' Creed and the Gloria, which are used frequently in worship; in spite of the epiclesis of the eucharistic prayer, which always calls on the Holy Spirit to sanctify these gifts of bread and wine; in spite of the prominent place of the Spirit in Calvin's eucharistic theology, the congregants interviewed simply did not use pneumatological language to describe their understanding or experience of communion. The Supper has to do with the first two persons of the Trinity, but the Holy Spirit is not part of the conscious eucharistic theology of the congregation.

This disjunction between the themes in the Great Prayer and themes articulated in interviews grows out of the complex nature of

19. But see below, note 26.

lex orandi: more than text, it includes performance, history, memory, and current lived experience of the worshipers. Taking all of these things into account, it is no surprise that some themes emerge as prominent in this congregation's primary theology, while others fade into the background. Because the performance of the whole eucharist focuses attention on the Words of Institution, for instance, events of Christ's earlier ministry and anticipation of his coming again are both marginalized. The "gift of Jesus Christ" for which people are thankful has primarily to do with the sacrificial gift of his life for the forgiveness of our sins. Primary theology is also shaped by histories of practice and catechesis, which vary according to congregation and individual worshiper. In this case, the absence of pneumatological language probably reflects a lack of attention to the role of the Holy Spirit in both church education and liturgical practice over a long period of time. Just because it is prayed earnestly in present practice does not mean that the Great Prayer immediately or automatically molds participants' lived experience. Once again, as with the invitation, a single liturgical element can support a variety of eucharistic theologies: while text elaborates a full Christology and trinitarian theology, juxtaposition of the prayer with the Words places more emphasis on the passion of Christ in the past, rather than pre-Passion ministry, the present work of the Holy Spirit, or the future hope: "until we feast with him in glory."

Remembering: The Words of Institution

The Great Prayer ends with the entire congregation praying the Lord's Prayer. After the "Amen," Matthew proceeds immediately to the Words of Institution. He recites these from memory, in the manner of someone relating a familiar story to a group of friends who have heard it many times before. As a result, the exact wording varies from communion to communion; on this particular occasion he says the following:

> With Christians around the world this day, we remember the night on which Jesus *(pause to pick up loaf)* took bread. Now after he blessed it, he broke it *(Matthew breaks bread and shows congregation),* and he gave it to his disciples saying, "This is my body

121

which is broken for you. Eat this in remembrance of me." *(Pause to put bread down)* We also remember how he took the cup *(Matthew pours the juice from pitcher into cup and holds up the cup)*, and after he had blessed it, he gave it to his disciples saying, "This cup is the new covenant in my blood, shed for you for the forgiveness of sins. Drink of it, all of you, "for as often as you eat this bread and drink this cup, you proclaim the Lord's death till he comes again." And so today we celebrate with brothers and sisters in Christ around the world this *big* meal.

The opening and closing ("With Christians around the world this day" and "And so today we celebrate . . .") relate directly to the emphasis of World Communion Sunday, integrating this liturgical element with the sermon and invitation. The Words of Institution themselves are a modified form of 1 Corinthians 11:23-26 [Luke 22:19-20], with interpolations from Matthew 26:27-28.[20] That is, the phrases "shed for you for the forgiveness of sins" and "drink of it, all of you" come from the Matthean version of the Last Supper, while the remainder of the institution narrative here comes more or less from the Corinthian version. This amalgam of scriptural references is not simply idiosyncratic; there has never been a single form of the Words of Institution prescribed for Presbyterian practice.[21] There are subtle variations in wording across American Presbyterianism, and even within the denomination's current *Book of Common Worship*, there are two different versions of the Words.[22] The variation peculiar to this pastor is the phrasing *"Eat* this in remembrance of me" rather than the usual *"Do* this in remembrance of me." This is particularly striking since "Do this in remembrance of me" is such a familiar text, frequently engraved on communion tables across the country and popping up repeatedly in interviews with members of

20. For a helpful comparison of the four institution narratives in the New Testament (Mark 14:22-25; Matthew 26:26-29; Luke 22:15-20; and 1 Corinthians 11:23-26), see Jasper and Cuming, *Prayers of the Eucharist*, pp. 16-18.

21. At certain times and places in history, however, certain forms of the Words were probably understood to be normative; as in the southern Presbyterian church (PCUS) in the early part of the twentieth century. The 1921 and 1945 editions of the *Book of Church Order* include identical versions of the Words, both reflecting and shaping general practice in the churches.

22. See *Book of Common Worship*, pp. 68, 70-71, and 74.

this congregation. The unusual phrasing has the effect, intended or not, of standing out in the hearer's ear and focusing on the act of eating the bread. The second "Do this in remembrance of me," after Jesus offers the cup in the Corinthian passage, is omitted altogether.

The minister here is not simply reciting the words, of course; he is enacting the gestures of Jesus at the Last Supper: breaking the bread, pouring the wine/juice, and holding them up for the congregation to see. These actions focus the congregation's attention even more strongly on the Last Supper, not just as the meal that originated the eucharist, but as an event that reaches into the present through the minister presiding at table.

The gestures of breaking and pouring help to draw attention to the Words of Institution as the focal point of the eucharist. But, as mentioned in the previous section, there are other aspects of this eucharistic performance that reinforce the prominence of the Words of Institution. The very fact that it is the pastor, and not the associate pastor, who consistently pronounces the Words at communion services in this church is a subtle clue to the importance of this element. Nor is it merely his official status as head of staff that lends his liturgical performance more force; Matthew also presents himself as more sure than Mark in the role of presider. He speaks clearly and forcefully, with energy that engages the worshiping congregation. Mark, by contrast, is more soft-spoken, and any evocative gestures he might employ during the prayers are largely missed by the congregation, who have their eyes closed. So Matthew's greater performative authority, as well as official authority, contribute to the centrality of the Words of Institution in this church's primary theology.

It is not simply contemporary practice, however, that focuses the congregation's attention on the Words of Institution as central act of the eucharist. It is also the history of practice in this place and this ecclesial tradition. While other aspects of the eucharist have changed over time — the eucharistic prayer, the method of distribution, the admission of children to the table — and while the exact Words shift according to minister and occasion, the basic pattern of the Words and their place immediately preceding distribution is a deeply embedded tradition here. It is probably the most consistent element in the entire eucharistic complex. This prominent use of the Words of Institution stems from the Reformed emphasis on biblical warrant in liturgical

123

and sacramental practice; since the sixteenth century, Reformed leaders have appealed to scripture as the norm shaping the worship of God. For this reason, the Words of Institution have occupied central place in Reformed eucharistic practice since the beginning. This long and consistent history of practice shapes the memory of the congregation so that they expect the Words of Institution to be the high point of the entire celebration. Memory and performance in this instance reinforce one another, feeding a strand of eucharistic theology that focuses on the Words of Institution as the center of the eucharist.

Present performance and history of emphasis on the Words of Institution together have formed the congregation in their attitude to the Lord's Supper, so that many experience it primarily as a time of recollecting the Last Supper of Christ. In the survey of the congregation, one question asked "What is the most important part of communion for you?" By far the most popular response to this was "the Words of Institution."[23] This response ranked above prayer, eating and drinking, or any other single act in the entire eucharistic complex — and by a wide margin. Clearly the Words are central to this congregation's lived experience of eucharist, a fact that coheres with the history and contemporary communion practice. But the survey also revealed a connection between a focus on the Words and the interpretation of eucharist as a reminder of the Last Supper. To the question "What is the meaning of the Lord's Supper for you?" the most popular overall response was "reminds us of the Last Supper of Jesus and his death."[24] Those who chose this response as the primary meaning of communion were more likely to choose "Words of Institution" as the central act of communion. These responses suggest that, for a large number of

23. Fifty-five out of 115 respondents, or nearly 50 percent, chose this answer as their first choice. Ironically, however, although the Words of Institution were chosen by most as the central act of communion, 1 Corinthians 11:23-26 was not the passage chosen by most respondents in answer to the question "What scripture passage is most helpful to you in thinking about communion?" The most popular answer to that question, by a sizable margin, was Matthew 26, only a small portion of which is included in the usual Words of Institution in this church.

24. When asked what the meaning of the Lord's Supper is, a majority of respondents ranked three as the first, second, or third most meaningful: "reminds us of the Last Supper of Jesus and his death" (86 percent), "unites us with the body of Christ" (84 percent), and "calls us into fellowship with each other" (56 percent). See Appendix 1, question 6.

people in this congregation, communion is experienced primarily as a time of recollecting the Last Supper of Christ.

This theme of remembrance appeared frequently in interviews as well. Of the thirty-five individuals interviewed, thirteen described communion as a "reminder" or a "time of remembrance," and when pressed for clarification, most explained that it was a reminder of Christ's Last Supper and/or death. Some actually used or paraphrased fragments of the institution narrative: "We *do it in remembrance of Christ*"; "We take this because Christ said to *do this in remembrance of him*"; "Jesus said *as often as you do this you show forth the Lord's death.*" These words have embedded themselves in the memories of these members, permanently shaping the way they interpret the action of the eucharist. Some other interviewees identified communion explicitly with the Last Supper. One man said, for example, "Communion is the celebration of the Last Supper, that Christ was here among us and that was the last time some of the disciples would see him." Those who described communion as a remembrance of the Last Supper tended to understand it as a somber time, shadowed by the awareness of death. One man, a POW during World War II, even compared the mood of communion services at First Presbyterian to the mood of a recent service of remembrance honoring military veterans who had died in the past year.

Remembering was also linked to sacrificial language for many congregants. Communion is "a remembrance of Christ *and his sacrifice*," according to one member of the congregation. Another commented, "Communion is the one time for remembering the *sacrifices* Christ made for us, and that because he did that, you truly are forgiven for what you have done." Remembering the Last Supper and Christ's sacrifice is a major complex of themes in the local eucharistic theology of this church.

Because of the prominence of the Words of Institution, both in the performance and in the lived experience of this congregation, other aspects of Christ's life and work are marginalized in the eucharist. Resurrection is important in the Great Prayer of Thanksgiving, and it occurs from time to time in hymns at communion, but the resurrection theme is all but absent from people's descriptions of what is going on in communion.[25] This is particularly ironic given Calvin's own under-

25. The one exception to this was a woman who quoted Christ's saying, "I am the

125

standing of the eucharist as an event in which the Spirit lifts up our very selves to join with Christ's resurrected and ascended body seated in glory at the right hand of the Father. Also marginalized in this congregation's eucharistic theology is attention to Christ's ministry before the Last Supper. Virtually all the "remembering" that goes on, according to the interviews, is remembering of Christ's last meal and crucifixion.[26] Again, this is despite the explicit anamnesis of Christ's entire life in the Great Prayer. This absence of reference to the resurrection or pre-Passion life of Jesus grows out of the long history of eucharistic practices and teachings in this church and many other Protestant churches. The fuller treatment of Christ's life and ministry simply has not been part of the eucharistic practice here long enough for it to have made a significant difference to the articulated theology of the congregation.

The emphasis on the Words of Institution in this church's practice affects the reception of the Great Prayer by the congregation so that both feed a modified "memorial meal" understanding of communion, not unlike that of Zwingli. This marginalizes other themes such as Christ's pre-Passion ministry, resurrection, and second coming. Having said all of this, however, is not to exhaust the primary eucharistic theology of this congregation. The Words by themselves do not end the eucharist; they necessarily lead into the distribution of the bread and wine/juice to the congregation. The story retold would not be sufficient; it opens to welcome all those baptized present to the table Jesus shared with his disciples. And this opening to the gathered assembly will bring us face to face with two diverse eucharistic theologies that co-exist in this congregation: one theological strand that focuses on the corporate sharing of the bread and wine/juice, and another that emphasizes the individual relationship with Christ through personal prayer and reception of the elements. The remainder of this chapter will address these two theological lenses on the eucharist.

---

living bread," and went on to comment, "Every other religion has a dead god; we have a living God."

26. The two notable exceptions to this were one woman's description of Christ as servant and a former Episcopalian's experience of communion as a part of the crowd watching Jesus perform a miracle.

Sharing: Distribution of the Elements

In this church, the Words of Institution lead directly into the distribution of the elements. Distribution is usually done by passing trays of bread and wine/juice down the pews, but occasionally the congregation is invited forward to receive communion by intinction. On this particular occasion, distribution is by pew. Once Matthew has concluded the institution narrative, he gestures for the elders to come to the table, where they receive the trays of bread to pass out to the congregation. Afterward they distribute the juice in the same manner, as described in greater detail in the prologue.

The method of distribution is a contested issue in this church, more contested than any other part of the communion service — probably because it is the only part that changes with any regularity. And the different methods of distribution embody and instill quite different primary theologies. Pew communion as practiced here cultivates an attitude of interiority and personal reflection. There is no verbal exchange between those serving and those receiving. People help themselves to bread and juice from the plates, with little or no assistance from their neighbors. The arrangement of pews in rows facing forward itself encourages an inward focus, since visual contact with others is minimal. All of this fosters an understanding of eucharist as individual reflection. I will discuss this attitude at greater length in the section on praying.

By contrast, methods of distribution that require more physical involvement of the participants foster greater attention to the gathered community. Let us return to the story I have cited in previous chapters about one congregation's shift in attitude that grew out of a shift from pew communion to intinction. When this happened, people in the front rows were able to see the faces of those behind them as they came down the aisle. They smiled in pleasure at one another. The liturgical phrases about the congregation as the "one body of Christ" and the table as a "joyful feast" assumed new meaning, because the congregation behaved more like one connected body, and there was a palpable joy in the gathering. In the congregation of this study, on the occasions when members go forward for communion, they too engage one another visually. All the participants are inescapably aware of the gathered community in a way that is not as evident during pew distribution. While not all congregants appreciated this mode of participation, the interviews reveal that nearly half prefer more physically engaged methods of distribution precisely because they generate more of a sense of community than sitting in the pew.[27]

"Something about lining up and going forward was very special [in childhood experiences of communion]," commented one interviewee. "I felt like more part of the process. . . . Seeing all the people going forward as well as going yourself — actually getting up and moving — made it special." Another man described intinction as more meaningful because "it involves me more with others taking communion." The presence of others participating in communion is crucial in his experience; "I wouldn't want to take it alone." And another man explicitly compared methods of distribution by saying that there is more "community feeling" going forward than staying in the pew. "In the pew you are more alone with your thoughts." Many interviewees, subtly or not so subtly, make this connection between going forward and understanding communion as a corporate act.

Others described communion services in which they took the elements in the pew, but which still carried the sense of communal celebration. One man, an adult convert to Christianity, described his first experiences of communion at a Presbyterian church in Texas. Plates of bread were passed, but the bread was not pre-cut; it was in loaves or, on at least one occasion, in the form of tortillas. Physical participation was emphasized, as people had to tear off pieces of bread. This meant that "your neighbor had to help you; you couldn't tear the bread by yourself." The minister in that church encouraged them to take big pieces with "gusto and delight." It definitely had the air of celebration. In that case, pew communion was explicitly described and understood as a corporate act.

Some interviewees and survey respondents who described communion in terms of community preferred the practice of pew communion in which all the congregants consume the elements at the same time. As with the practice of going forward to receive the elements, those who preferred consuming the bread and wine all together un-

---

27. Seventeen of thirty-five interviewees described communion as a corporate celebration, an act of the community. This is exactly the same number that described communion as a private, individual act.

derstood this to be an expression of the church's unity. "Taking bread and wine at the same time emphasized the whole church together," reflected one interviewee. "There is more individual focus when we each take it separately." A former Baptist agreed, saying that in her former church, "communion was always passed and taken at the same time. . . . I prefer that method, because you commune with God more when you all are thinking together."[28]

Receiving the elements, whether in the pew or at the front of the sanctuary, is but one side of the process of distribution. Serving is also a central part of the eucharist for some participants. In the Presbyterian system, members of the congregation, and traditionally, ordained elders, serve the bread and wine/juice to the rest of the congregation.[29] In alternative settings such as retreats, communion may be celebrated in a circle in which each person serves the bread and wine to her neighbor. Several of those interviewed described this act of serving communion in terms of relationship to the community. For instance, one elder reflected that "serving communion is very different from taking it in the pew. . . . I see the elements less in terms of food and more in terms of faith. Food might be a representation of love to the community." Another elder, who came to Christianity as an adult, spoke excitedly about learning to serve communion at an elders' retreat: "I had no idea that you are actually *serving* the person next to you. . . . A lot of people don't know that you take it and you hand it to the other person, serve yourself and then [that person] turns around and serves the next person. Serving your neighbor is important." For these elders and others, the experience of serving reinforces the understanding of communion as a corporate act because it involves the server directly with those being served.

28. According to the survey, 36 percent of the congregation who expressed a preference would rather receive the communion elements in the pews; 34 percent preferred going forward and receiving the elements from a minister; 7 percent preferred passing the bread and cup around a circle; and 5 percent preferred intinction. So although a slim majority favor pew communion if each option is considered separately, the other three more active methods of distribution considered together make up a clear majority (46 percent).

29. There is now a provision in the Book of Order for any church member to serve communion if invited by the session (W-3616.d.). It is still the norm, however, for ordained elders to distribute the elements in this local church.

Whether serving or receiving, in the pew or by intinction, more physical engagement in the act of communion is clearly linked to a greater awareness of and appreciation for the gathered community as central to the sacrament. This strand of *lex orandi* emerges both from observation and from listening to the history and current experience of congregants. In this congregation, this theological strand exists side by side with another strand of primary theology that focuses on the individual and her engagement in personal prayer.

Praying: Reflection During Distribution

In the particular communion service considered here, people do not leave their pews to receive the elements. The elders come quietly down the aisles to their assigned places and pass the trays of bread and juice to the congregants, who are trying to decide when, what, and whether to sing. As noted in the prologue, congregational singing during distribution is not the normal practice here; it is an experiment on this day to encourage greater congregational participation during the serving of elements. The newness of the practice and the unannounced decisions of the organist to omit two of the four hymns and play an extended interlude before the final verse of another hymn all worked against the intention, creating more confusion than community.

But the confusion itself points to the fact that this practice is not the usual method of distributing the elements. People are accustomed to sitting quietly and hearing soft organ music while the bread and juice are passed, allowing for a time of individual prayer. And many place great value on such a time of prayer, even interpreting that as the main point of communion. This is best summed up in the words of one younger woman in the congregation, who repeated her mother's description of communion as her "quiet time with Jesus." For these folks, the actions of passing the bread and wine/juice or walking down the aisles to receive communion are distractions from the real work of eucharist, which is prayer. Thirty percent of the survey respondents said that "private individual prayer" was the most important part of communion. And of the thirty-five individuals interviewed, seventeen described communion in personal, individual terms: "the point of communion is personal reflection"; "I would like communion to be a private introspective type of thing"; "I look forward to my communion for this prayerful time." Over and over, people with this perspective on communion describe other actions as distracting: "You should close your eyes and bow your head and think about what it *is*. . . . Serving can distract from that, as well as trying to sing during communion." Two different choir members indicated that singing in the choir during the distribution of elements can also be distracting, because it interferes with personal meditation.[30]

Closely tied to this understanding of communion as a time of meditation is a distinction between "meaning" and "doing." That is, the people who want to "tune out the world" and pray during communion also tend to describe the real "meaning" of communion as something separate from the actions. "I try not to think about the way it's done and think about what it *is*," said one woman emphatically when I asked her about her preferred mode of participating in communion. Another said, "Taking communion in other places makes me focus more on what I'm supposed to *do* rather than the real *meaning*." A younger man who recently attended eucharist at an Episcopal church reflected similarly: "I had no time to react to the true *meaning* because I was so nervous about *doing* things right."[31] The "meaning" of communion is something primarily accessible through quiet meditation. "Doing" too much gets in the way, especially if it is unfamiliar doing, like attending a new church or trying to serve communion for the first time.[32]

30. Ironically, this devotional mode of participation in eucharist is reminiscent of medieval devotions during liturgical rites, when many lay participants did not regularly partake of the elements.

31. Of course, there is a difference between (1) an ongoing separation of meaning from doing and (2) the obstacle to participation posed by a liturgy that is unfamiliar or distracting. The interviewees who expressed concern about doing things right in a new setting reflect, in part, Calvin's own concern for engagement of the worshiper in order for sacramental participation to be effective. Even so, it is significant that the language these congregants chose to express their concern relied on a split between meaning and doing.

32. This separation of meaning and doing resembles Calvin's insistence on the separation of "sign" and "thing" in his eucharistic theology. Calvin argued that we must raise our thoughts from material things to the heavenly things they signify; otherwise, we risk getting caught up in idolatry. Members of this congregation who focus on individual prayer would largely agree with Calvin's concern, but they seem to go even farther: not only do they want to separate themselves from the material things,

For those who articulate this view, the preferred method of receiving communion is to pass the trays of pre-cut bread and the separate glasses of grape juice down the pews.[33] A minimum of movement allows for more individual reflection. "[Intinction] didn't mean as much as sitting in the pew and being able to pray as I ate and drank," reflected one man. Another man, who actually preferred communion by intinction because of its community feeling, admitted that "the only thing I miss with intinction is the personal moment or space. . . . There is no moment for prayer before eating with intinction."[34]

Like too much "doing," celebrating communion too frequently also detracts from its "meaning," according to several representatives of this perspective. "Weekly communion makes it less special," was the consensus of eight interviewees. They share a concern that celebrating too often makes people stop thinking about what they are doing. "If you aren't careful, weekly communion can become thoughtless," said one. Meaning depends on thought. Again, the point of communion is equated with individual reflection, something that is jeopardized by extraneous activity or repetition.

---

but they also want to separate themselves from contact with other people. This directly contradicts Calvin's concern for the social dimension of the eucharist.

33. Of the people interviewed, six of thirty-five, or 17 percent, explicitly preferred pew communion over any other method. Of the survey respondents who answered the question "Which mode of communion in which you have participated was most meaningful to you?" 36 percent answered that they preferred pew communion — the largest single response to that question.

34. It is ironic that pew communion has developed this strong sense of interiority and individual reflection. As Donald Baillie points out in one lecture on the eucharist, the Reformed tradition has been noted for its corporate focus as enacted in the serving of the elements to one another in the pew: "When we Presbyterians celebrate communion we do not go up individually to the altar; we sit in our places together as at the Lord's table. We are gathered at the family board for a feast in fellowship, we pass the bread and the cup from hand to hand, receiving them from our neighbour and passing them on to our neighbour in the communion of the Lord's supper. What excuse then have we for forgetting that this is indeed a corporate act, a meal in sacred fellowship, an anticipation of 'the marriage supper of the Lamb'?" (Donald Baillie, "The Eucharistic Offering," in *The Theology of the Sacraments and Other Papers* [New York: Charles Scribner's Sons, 1957], p. 123). Whereas this was certainly the intent of the practice, and may indeed have been the lived theology at one time, it is clearly the case that in this congregation, the practice of pew communion fosters an individual rather than a corporate focus.

Clearly, a particular practice of distribution has contributed to a eucharistic theology that de-emphasizes the corporate body and focuses on the individual's personal relationship with Christ through prayer. The point of eucharistic practice is its "meaning," discernment of which demands personal effort, and which can be obscured by too much "doing." Though praying and sharing are not mutually exclusive dimensions of eucharist, in this place they seem to function as competing, rather than complementary, theologies.

Two Eucharistic Theologies

Inviting, thanking, remembering, sharing, praying: these five actions make up the basic movement of the communion service in this congregation. Taken together, they make up a fairly full eucharistic theology, one that echoes many aspects of the Reformed theological tradition. But it would be misleading to synthesize too quickly the practices and perspectives represented here as if they were one undifferentiated whole. This theological interpreter has to acknowledge that she is faced with a fractured ritual act. Emerging from this mass of observation, textual analysis, survey data, and interviews are two broad approaches to the eucharist, two local theologies existing simultaneously in this congregation. They are not entirely separate; as noted above, each liturgical element operates on multiple levels, so that it can feed more than one theological strand. And a specific church member may not be committed to a single eucharistic theology, but may articulate aspects of both perspectives. Nevertheless, when interpreted as a whole, the eucharistic practice in this congregation yields two different theologies: one that centers on the act of individual prayer, and the other that centers on the corporate sharing of the elements. The first approach focuses on individual praying and turns participants' attention away from embodied participation in the eucharistic ritual. The second focuses on corporate sharing and orients participants toward their engagement in the ritual act.

Lord's Supper as Individual Devotion

As mentioned already, the usual practice of pew communion in this church orients the individual inward, encouraging an attitude of personal prayer. Members of the congregation sit quietly as the trays are passed, serving themselves the elements in silence. The arrangement of pews in rows facing forward itself encourages an inward focus, since visual contact with others in the congregation is minimal.

A particular kind of music also contributes to a more inward experience of eucharist. Although the communion service detailed in the prologue involved congregational singing of hymns during the distribution, the uncertainty of participation on that occasion revealed the congregation's deep ambivalence about this practice. Rather than singing, the musical accompaniment to distribution in this church has usually been soft organ music. This is the type of music preferred by the vast majority of survey respondents.[35] Soft organ music in this place tends not to draw attention to itself, but serves as a cover for the sounds of the elders serving the elements so that those in the pews can focus on personal prayer. All of these ritual practices lead the practitioners to focus inward, away from the external ritual acts. But notice: members of the congregation are engaged in ritual activity here. The actions are minimal, not grand, but they are ritual actions nonetheless. This is a point to which we will return: this strand of eucharistic theology that focuses on individual devotion, not on external action, is itself nurtured by a particular set of ritual actions.

Another practice that contributes to this strand of eucharistic theology is the barring of children from the table until confirmation. As mentioned in the section on invitation, it was only in the 1970s and early 1980s that Presbyterian churches began to admit baptized children to the table, understanding eucharistic participation as a part of the church's nurture of its youngest members. Before that shift in practice, confirmation was the event at which children were invited to partake of communion, after they had made a public profession of

35. To the survey question regarding preferred instrumentation during communion, 86 percent of respondents indicated that they prefer organ or piano alone. To the question about mood of music preferred, 86 percent also responded that the music ought to be "quiet and reflective."

faith and been examined by the session. This practice reinforced the idea that communion requires a certain level of intellectual understanding for participation. This theme appeared repeatedly in interviews: "Communion was a special privilege for those old enough to understand"; "I assumed that . . . you needed to understand the significance of the whole thing and that they didn't really teach you that until after you got in [confirmation class], and so therefore you really weren't qualified to take communion." It is striking that the interviewees who were not barred from the table as children did not separate "meaning" from "doing," and they did not tend to describe the sacrament in individual, personal terms. Placing such a strong emphasis on the "age of discernment" as the qualification for communion certainly coheres with Calvin's emphasis on "discerning the body" as a necessary aspect of full participation in communion.[36] But it has had the effect, over time, of making a certain intellectual capacity a prerequisite to communion. Understanding the meaning of communion, for many, requires quiet, focused attention to God in individual prayer. In this way, the practice of keeping baptized children from the table until confirmation, together with the set of communion practices that turned the participants inward, contributed to a eucharistic theology that presents communion as an individual act of discerning meaning which overlooks the set of practices on which it is based.

Interviews with members of the congregation revealed that many have been shaped by these practices to regard individual prayer as the most important part of communion. This group prefers modes of outward participation that give ample space for personal meditation: pew communion celebrated infrequently, refraining from singing, even being served rather than serving. These practices allow participants to focus on the real "meaning" of communion rather than the outward "doing."[37]

Ritual theorists such as Ronald Grimes point out that it is misleading to focus exclusively on "meaning" when analyzing a particular rit-

---

36. Though, as mentioned above in note 8, this practice of waiting until the "age of discernment" for eucharistic participation was not an invention of Calvin's.

37. To be sure, this attitude can also be quite demanding of the individual, focusing on the internal realization of union with Christ. The "doing," in this approach to eucharist, is almost all interior.

ual. When he was asked to respond to a major study of U.S. Roman Catholic liturgical changes twenty-five years after Vatican II, Grimes pointed out that the study "attends primarily to the exegetical meaning of symbols (that is, what people say about those symbols) and it ignores their operational and positional meanings."[38] Symbols have more than "exegetical meaning," Grimes argues; they have meaning that emerges from the way they function in a given context. This is the "emergent quality" of ritual discussed in chapter three above. Meaning does not exist independently of ritual practice, but grows out of it. Any ritual study needs to take account of this emergent quality in performed ritual. For example, we have explored earlier the way the Words of Institution serve as focal point of the communion service, influencing the way the eucharistic prayer is heard. This emphasis could not be discerned from analysis of text alone, but only in performance — and especially when that performance is supplemented by interpretations by congregational members. "Meaning" in the text is multiplex, but emergent meaning has a narrower focus.

In another example, the distribution of elements has a set of official meanings articulated by the denomination's Directory for Worship: thanksgiving, remembering, invocation, communion of the faithful, and foretaste of the kingdom meal.[39] In practice, however, meaning emerges partly out of the particular way distribution is done. The meaning of pew communion in the sanctuary is not identical to the meaning of communion shared in a circle by a lake at an elders' retreat. There are similarities, but there are also differences that need to be taken seriously.

Having said all of this, however, and acknowledging with Grimes that meaning is context-dependent, it is nevertheless the case that many people in this congregation rely on a separation of "meaning" and "doing" for their interpretations of eucharist. When asked about preferred location for communion or preferred modes of taking communion, many of this group responded as one woman did: "I try to separate myself from the surroundings," or "I try not to think about

38. Ronald Grimes, "Liturgical Renewal and Ritual Criticism," in *The Awakening Church: Twenty-five Years of Liturgical Renewal*, ed. Lawrence J. Madden, S.J. (Collegeville, Minn.: Liturgical Press, 1992), p. 18.

39. See Directory for Worship in the *Book of Order* (Louisville: Presbyterian Church [USA], 2005-2007), W-2.4003-7.

the way it's done and think about what it *is*." The meaning is independent of the action, according to this view.

Significantly, although this group articulates a gap between "meaning" and "doing," it seems clear that this position grows out of a particular set of practices, a particular network of "doings." And ironically, though many interviewees shared the perspective that meaning has little to do with the way communion is done, these same respondents often went on to say that they preferred pew communion because it enables them to focus on meaning rather than doing. There is a correlation between a focus on "meaning" and certain practices that nurture internal reflection.

This view of the Lord's Supper as individual devotion, I suggest, represents one strand within the Reformed tradition: the tendency to regard symbolic action as risky, requiring proper interpretation for right participation. One has to understand the meaning before engaging in the doing. Right doctrine precedes right practice. This is the general tendency I am trying to challenge in my own proposal. The interesting correlation that has emerged in studying this particular congregation is that the group that articulates a separation of meaning and doing, that separates interpretation from practice, depends on and favors a particular set of practices, and a history of such practices.

This view of communion illustrates the point made by Edward Muir, cited in chapter three: that the legacy of the Reformation is that rituals no longer present something; they *re*-present something. The focus is on hermeneutics, on meaning. Rather than engaging us in a reality, rituals point to a reality that exists elsewhere.[40] The ironic twist suggested by the present study is that this hermeneutical approach to sacraments depends on a particular set of practices for its existence.

Lord's Supper as Corporate Action

Although the usual practice of pew communion in this congregation turns participants inward, focusing on individual discernment of meaning, there are also times when the eucharist draws people out

40. See Edward Muir, *Ritual in Early Modern Europe* (Cambridge: Cambridge University Press, 1997), pp. 7-8, 150; see also chapter three above.

into engagement with one another. During the congregational responses of the Sanctus and the Memorial Acclamation during the eucharistic prayer, for instance, people are physically joined through their corporate song and speech. Also, some eucharistic occasions involve participants in more overt ritual action. When this congregation celebrated communion on the Baptism of the Lord Sunday, the communion service was integrated with a corporate reaffirmation of baptismal vows, and members came forward to receive both the bread and wine/juice *and* an anointing with oil. This communion service had an abundance of ritual action. Fuller ritual engagement tends to lead people into greater awareness of the community around them. And the movement goes in the other direction as well: those who describe the eucharist as a corporate event tend to prefer celebrations that are more ritually full.

As I suggested above in the discussion of the distribution practices of this church, there is a large group at First Presbyterian who understand and experience communion as a celebration of community. According to one, "Communion is a chance to be together and share experience as a community." Interviewees with this perspective compared communion to family gatherings, to a cocktail party, to coming home. Communion requires the presence of other people, and it is enhanced when the people gathered actually know each other.

Members who shared this interpretation of communion also tended to prefer more active forms of participation. "More congregational participation in liturgy preparing for communion would be nice," commented one woman. "It is good to be involved." This woman also pointed out that visual contact in worship is important, because it enables each person to feel more involved with the whole group. This contrasts sharply with the view of the Lord's Supper as individual devotion, which says, "You should close your eyes and bow your head and think about what it *is*." Rather, for this group, the ritual actions of communion are directly related to the corporate understanding of communion.

Those who described communion as corporate celebration also favored going forward to receive the elements or taking the elements all together in the pew, as I have already suggested. And they emphasized the act of serving as important because it fosters relationships rather than simply interfering with individual prayer. Two elders, both of them men who serve communion and also usher on a regular basis, commented that the practice of serving communion at First Presbyterian is no different from ushering. In both instances, the only direction they receive is "stage direction"; there is no reflection on the way in which serving the bread and wine/juice fosters community. They implied that serving communion ought to be — and for these two really *was* — an enactment of corporate celebration. The ritual action of serving was not to be effaced, but celebrated.

As the comments of these two men suggest, not only did this group prefer more overt ritual action, but they also tended to see that action as contributing to their particular theological interpretation of communion. So the contrast is twofold: the two groups prefer different levels of participation, and they understand the relationship between practice and interpretation differently. Those who understand the eucharist as individual devotion prefer minimal ritual activity, and they also tend to describe meaning as separate from doing. Those who understand the eucharist as corporate activity, on the other hand, prefer more overt ritual activity, and they also tend to emphasize the link between the meaning and the doing.

The contrast between these two views shows itself clearly in the varying perspectives of congregational members. But it would be a mistake to think that this is simply a matter of individual interpretation. The contrast between these two views is a contrast between two theologies inherent in the eucharistic performance itself. A history of keeping people from the table until they reach an age of intellectual maturity coupled with contemporary practice that emphasizes quiet prayer and downplays human interaction sends the signal that the central elements in eucharist are the individual and Jesus Christ: "my quiet time with Jesus." In this version of theology, embodied actions are muted, drawing the attention of participants inward in intense personal reflection. Side by side with this is the set of practices that engage worshipers in more outward activity: walking forward, seeing other members of the community, singing, tearing pieces of bread. These eucharistic movements foreground the body as central to the liturgical action. In this theological stream, the presence of others is foregrounded as well, so that the community becomes central to the liturgy. The congregation at First Presbyterian experiences both sorts of communion practices, some more focused on inward devotion and some more focused on outward, corporate activity. In this way, two different theologies are fostered in the life of the congregation.

Conclusion

At one level, this case study is an illustration of how to take seriously local eucharistic practice in order to see how *lex orandi* gives rise to *lex credendi*. Here I have tried to unpack local practice both from the outside (through ritual and textual analysis) and from the inside (through interviews and surveys). From this it has become clear that the local *lex orandi* itself is not uniform; there is variety in the way eucharist is celebrated, as well as a contrast in leadership styles between the two ministers. Furthermore, there has been a significant shift in communion practices over the last couple of decades. Add to this the fact that the congregation itself comes from a variety of denominational backgrounds, and it is no surprise that the local understanding of eucharist, the local *lex credendi,* is not uniform. As a result of this limited study, we may say that in general, members of this congregation have one of two perspectives on the eucharist: either it is a time of individual prayer and discernment of meaning, or it is a public celebration of the corporate body of Christ.

By lifting out these two theological streams from my congregational study, I do not intend to ignore the theological richness and complexity of this local *lex orandi*. I hope that my examination of the themes of inviting, thanking, and remembering indicate some of the other crucial themes that emerged from the various forms of congregational analysis.[41] The basic contrast between corporate sharing and in-

---

41. Many other themes could be explored, in this congregation or in other congregations, as a result of this initial study. For instance, one could focus on the sub-practices of introspection: although those who understand the Lord's Supper as individual devotion may not focus on their own practices, one could explore more deeply what particular practices facilitate this devotional attitude. One might also fruitfully investigate what exactly people are meditating on when they meditate during communion: Are they devoting their energies to awareness of sin and guilt? Grace and gratitude? With regard to those who understand the Supper as corporate action, one might explore the varieties that exist within this group: Are some focused especially on formation of the local community, while others are more focused on connection with the

dividual praying, however, illuminates the larger tension I have been trying to address throughout this project: the tension within the Reformed theological tradition with regard to ritual practice, a tension that has been weighted in one direction for much of Reformed history.

This disagreement over the status of ritual and symbolic action, illustrated by the competing eucharistic theologies in this particular church, may be stated as follows: Is communion a secondary acting out of a more basic understanding — a doing that is subsequent to meaning? Or is communion a "symbol which gives rise to thought," to use Paul Ricoeur's language, a ritual event that leads to theological interpretation? In this congregation, those who tend to interpret the Supper as individual devotion describe ritual action as secondary to doctrine. They distinguish between the "symbol" of communion and the reality to which it points, displaying some anxiety about the power of symbols to lead to problematic doctrines. For instance, one woman was even uncomfortable with the words "This *is* my body." She reflected that it would be more "accurate and appropriate" to say "This *is symbolic of* my body broken for you." From her perspective, to value ritual too highly confuses the material elements with God. The term "symbolic" helped her to distinguish God from the material realm. This approach coheres with a set of practices that have taught people for generations that communion is an adult event, open to those with a certain intellectual capacity, and have primarily to do with discerning the invisible meaning beyond the visible symbols.

But from the perspective of those who see the Supper as corporate event, confusion of God with the material realm is not the danger. Instead, the danger is that we will not fully appreciate the mystery of the incarnation. So another woman commented, "I don't think it's just symbolic. . . . [Jesus] said, 'I am the bread of life,' and we're taking the bread of life into us. I try to think of it as real and not just symbolic." In this case, the ritual action is more closely identified with the action of God. The practice itself is more highly valued, and it is not second-

---

larger church? Are some of them simply devoted to the experience of communion, while others experience eucharist as an ethical imperative to care for the world? Finally, with both groups, one might explore the ways in which scripture forms their imaginations in different ways. Are there, like Luther and Zwingli, particular passages that emerge as formative of each group's theology, or are there a variety of scriptural texts shaping each position? How does scripture work to mold each of these perspectives?

ary to doctrine. This view of practice as formative of understanding (rather than secondary to understanding) was suggested in one interviewee's comment that "worship ought to provoke thought — that makes it alive." Those in the congregation who understand communion in particular as a communal event also understand ritual practice generally as formative and transformative of persons.

The latter position, I contend, is the strand of the Reformed tradition that we need to reclaim today. The resources are present in the tradition, in Calvin himself as well as in the writings of subsequent Reformed theologians such as John Williamson Nevin. And, as this congregational study suggests, some congregational members adopt this stance with regard to the Lord's Supper. These members appreciate the way that communion in particular and ritual practice in general "provokes thought," forming them in faith. This lesser-known strand in the Reformed tradition deserves attention today, because it draws attention to the ways that God acts in and through the ordinary material stuff of life, through the breaking of bread and the drinking of juice, the bowing of heads and lifting of voices in song. The point is not simply whether eucharist itself is an individual act or a corporate one; the point is whether worshipers encounter the triune God as a living and active presence in and through the liturgical act, or as a presence primarily available through the act of interpretation. As I will suggest in the final chapter, what God does in and through full eucharistic participation is to form persons in more than cognitive understanding, and in more than emotionally uplifting appreciation of "meaning." Rather, it is formation in character and will that require bodily participation. As we engage more fully in eucharistic practice, affirming the ways God works in and through this ritual activity, the Holy Spirit may shape us to reflect God's glory more adequately, may lift us up to unite more closely with the body of Jesus Christ.

CHAPTER 5

A Ritual Approach to
Reformed Eucharistic Theology

In this project I have tried to argue that American Reformed Christians today need to take more seriously the event of the eucharist as a location for the activity of God. Although this theme has been sometimes muted and sometimes prominent in Reformed thought, it is a theme that deserves attention today, when many tend to think of eucharist as secondary acting out of a prior belief. Liturgical theologians and some contemporary ritual theorists have helped focus attention on the ritual doing of eucharist as a primary event of divine–human encounter. All of these disciplines contribute to a ritual approach to Reformed eucharistic theology.

What is "a ritual approach to Reformed eucharistic theology"? There are two related questions bound up in this phrase: first, what does it mean to do eucharist? And second, what does it mean to do theology? I will address them separately, but I hope the discussion will show how deeply the two are connected.

What Does It Mean to Do Eucharist?

"What is the Lord's Supper?" asks the Westminster Larger Catechism. In the introduction, I criticized Westminster's response to this question for being insufficiently attentive to actual eucharistic practice. After forays into historical Reformed theology, liturgical theology, ritual studies, and congregational analysis, we must now return to this question to attempt another sort of answer.

143

In the eucharist, our whole selves and Christ's whole self meet one another at a common table. This radical statement is at the heart of a ritual approach to eucharistic theology. The eucharist is an event that does not require our prior conceptual understanding, nor is it an event that is simply a human act. It is an act of divine self-manifestation in and through the words and symbols of the sacrament, received by faith. By the power of the Holy Spirit, those who come to the table with a taste of faith encounter and receive not just bread and wine, but the living Christ. To emphasize the ritual aspect of eucharist is to take seriously the human need for the visible and tangible, and also to honor the freedom of God to work through the visible and tangible as well as the audible elements of the eucharist. It is also to take seriously the fullness of Christ's humanity as well as his divinity. Both Calvin and Nevin describe the eucharist in this way, emphasizing Christ's presence in sacrament as well as Word, in symbolic objects and actions as well as doctrines. Calvin more than Nevin emphasized the freedom of God as crucial to understanding the way believers are joined to Christ in the eucharist. Nevin more than Calvin focused on the full humanity of Christ and the union of his natures, so that believers are joined not just to his divinity, but also to his humanity. But both theologians were concerned to counter the depiction of the eucharist as either a human rite attesting to our belief or an event in which God communicates only with human minds and memories rather than whole selves.

Calvin's principle of the unity of Word and sacrament and Nevin's emphasis on the unity of Christ's humanity and divinity both focus on the embodied eucharist as a place where, by the Spirit, believers encounter the living Christ, not just an act of conscious memory or his disincarnate divine nature. Although Calvin also directed his polemics against a localized understanding of Christ's presence, his insistence that Word and sacrament belong together serves to remind us that the Christ we encounter in eucharist by the power of the Spirit is the Word who was made flesh. To talk about Word without acknowledging sacrament is to risk changing the Word into words. Word is incarnate. This side of Calvin's theology is helpfully retrieved by the lens of ritual theory, which insists that words cannot be divorced from performance. A ritual approach to eucharistic theology keeps this ever in mind.

Eucharist, like all elements of the liturgy, is best understood as both anthropological rite and divine self-manifestation.[1] But these two aspects are not separate from one another. A ritual approach to eucharist, in attending to the anthropological rite, can, ironically, lead to a greater appreciation of eucharist as divine self-manifestation, because it establishes some distance between ourselves and the event, reassessing it as something that is ours and yet not-ours, a place where God promises to go ahead of us and meet us without our first having to explain how this is so.

In claiming that God acts in and through the eucharistic event, I am not arguing for a revamped metaphysical presence of Christ in the elements. Rather, as both Calvin and Nevin have suggested, God's Spirit works mysteriously in the eucharistic transaction between a community of receptive persons and the Word proclaimed and embodied. The role of receptivity is crucial here.[2] Faith is the necessary recipient of God's work in the eucharist, because as Calvin put it, elements are not converted; people are converted.[3] Faith as "active receptivity" must not be confused with an utter passivity that is unresponsive to any of God's action. Faith does respond. But as Calvin and, even more strongly, Nevin, insisted, faith is not the effective power of the eucharist. Like reason, faith must be understood as secondary to God's action. Furthermore, faith itself is formed by God's action; it is itself a gift of the Spirit, not a self-generated state. In two senses, then, is faith secondary to God's initiative: faith is formed by God's action and, once formed, it is the recipient of God's action.

God's action in the sacrament is what Calvin designated as the Holy Spirit. The Holy Spirit lifts faithful people into the presence of Christ and engrafts them into Christ's body, to use Calvin's own language. This happens in the context of community: the Holy Spirit works through a community to mold it more and more into a particular instantiation of the body of Christ. Through that community, indi-

1. Don Saliers, see above chapter two, p. 62.

2. For a helpful recent study of "active receptivity" as the appropriate way to construe human "sacramental doing," drawing particularly from Luther and Bonhoeffer, see Todd B. Murken, *Take and Eat, and Take the Consequences: How Receiving the Lord's Supper Is an Action That Makes a Difference* (New York: Peter Lang, 2002), esp. chapters 4, 6, and 7.

3. *Institutes* 4.17.15.

viduals are formed in active faith — and this too is the work of the Spirit. Active faith is thus prepared to receive the gift of the eucharist. Yet we must not presume to know in advance how the Spirit will work in the eucharist; in this respect, we can learn from ritual and performance theorists who emphasize the emergent quality of performed ritual. Specific meaning is context-dependent. To be sure, it would be a mistake to collapse pneumatology into performance theory, equating the work of the Spirit with emergent meaning in ritual in general. Nevertheless, the concept of emergence does illumine a quality of the Spirit that merits attention: namely, the mystery and freedom of the Spirit to act in each community in ways humans cannot predict or control.

When participants come to table with a taste of faith and encounter the presence of Christ, they can be bound to each other and to God in new ways. Seeing the eucharist through the lens of ritual theory alerts us to the ways in which it can establish and also challenge social relations. In Calvin, the Reformed tradition has a theologian who focused on the "we" in liturgical formulations. He described the purpose of the eucharist as the joining of the whole community of faith to one another and to Christ. As has already been said, Calvin's eucharistic interest was more social than metaphysical. But more can be said. We cannot simply assert that this happens as if it were some magical transformation that occurs independently of the act itself. That would be to fall into the same error that plagued Turretin and Hodge: the radical separation of "sign" and "matter."[4] Sign and matter must be related without being identical.

Approaching the eucharist as a ritual event holds sign and matter in a tensive but open relationship, avoiding the pitfalls of local presence on the one hand (identification of sign and matter) and trivialization of the sacrament on the other (utter separation of sign and matter). If the eucharist is regarded as ritual, then the sense of "sign" itself is expanded to include the entire event, rather than solely the material objects of bread and wine. "Sign" then cannot be reified, be-

4. These terms are used by Calvin to denote the material element of a sacrament (sign) and that which is conveyed by the sign (Christ, the "matter" or "substance"). (See for instance *Institutes* 4.14.15f.) While this relation is similar to contemporary discussions of "sign" and "signified," I use Calvin's terminology to avoid the appearance that I am endorsing any contemporary theory of signification.

cause it is slightly different on each occasion. The participants them-selves, together with their actions and attitudes, become signs. Be-cause the pattern of each human life is subtly different at each eucharistic occasion, what is received, by the individuals and by the community, is ever new. Even if the "matter," Christ, is constant, nev-ertheless the particular work of Christ in each eucharist will vary be-cause the sign varies.[5] The example of the eucharistic celebration in the movie "Priest," described in chapter three, illustrates this point. In that event, the "sign" was not just the bread and wine, but the transac-tion of Lisa and Father Greg: she receiving and he serving the ele-ments. In this transaction, Christ's forgiveness was manifested, and Lisa and Greg were bound together in a new relationship. To say sim-ply that in the eucharist we are joined with Christ is to miss the partic-ularity of how this happens in real local eucharistic celebrations. The claim of union without attention to actual practice is an abstraction from the concreteness of the eucharistic meal, which requires food and company gathered around a table.

Furthermore, it is important to regard the work of God in the eucharist over time. Eucharistic celebrations are not simply discon-nected events that bear accidental resemblance to one another. They are non-identical, but they are nevertheless repetition. As the inter-views in chapter four attest, it is the formation of persons over time that is the most profound effect of the eucharist. It is no accident that many interviewees, when asked about memorable or significant com-munion services, responded that they could not recall any single com-munion events that were especially memorable; it was the cumulative effect of celebrating the eucharist over a lifetime that formed them in particular attitudes. One man, who now approaches eucharist with wonder and gratitude, reflected that he used to be disappointed in communion experiences, because he expected something dramatic to happen. He wrestled with his own guilt before communion, and then he found that guilt increased because he did not feel anything change

---

5. This is similar to Catherine Pickstock's description of the eucharist as "non-identical repetition," which avoids the two extremes of false separation and confusion of finite and transcendent. See *After Writing: On the Liturgical Consummation of Philoso-phy* (Oxford: Blackwell Publishers, 1998), p. 160; the idea of non-identical repetition also appears in her discussion of Plato's *Phaedrus* (pp. 18, 25) and in her critiques of Derrida (pp. 35, 109).

in him at the table. But gradually, over years of practice and reflection, he came to an utterly different attitude. While he could not say when or how it happened, his perspective shifted so that he ends up in awe now each time the church celebrates communion, because he regards it as such a gift.

The gradual nature of God's work in the eucharist is also attested by congregants, both those who understood the eucharist as individual devotion and those who understood it as corporate celebration, who reflected on their childhood experiences of communion participation. One young woman, a former Episcopalian, grew up participating in eucharist weekly, going forward to the priest and receiving a blessing even before she was allowed to receive the elements. This deeply affected her approach to eucharist; even now, in a congregation that usually takes communion in the pews, she experiences it as a communal event and is more apt to look around at her neighbors as integral parts of the event rather than distractions from individual meditation. In contrast to this, an older woman and lifelong Southern Presbyterian confessed that her lifetime of practice had formed her in such a way that she focuses on interior reflection at communion. She had no specific memory of communion, either growing up or as an adult, because it has all been so similar: "the communion service is so standard and set: words of institution and elders coming forward. Nothing really unusual stands out even over a lifetime." But from her description it is clear that her paradigm of communion, reinforced by a lifetime of repetition, involves the elements served by elders and taken quietly in the pews. This practice has formed her in an attitude of individual prayer. As these examples illustrate, although some worshipers tended to regard eucharist as an individual event while others regarded it as more corporate, it was not a single event that shaped their attitudes in these ways. A pattern of eucharistic celebration inculcated these bodily and affective attitudes over a long period of time.

This, of course, leads to the question of adequate use, of what eucharistic practices form persons and communities more appropriately over time. This is the critical question addressed in chapter two in the discussion of liturgical theology. How do we move from descriptive to normative concerns without abandoning careful attention to local context and practice? Although a full answer to this question lies beyond the bounds of this project, certain points are emerging. Above all, normative criteria must come not only from outside, but from within the eucharist as celebrated by a local community. In particular, criteria of adequate use can be drawn from the eucharist's meal context, which implies that the bread and wine should be recognizable food and drink, that the company of others be central and not peripheral to the act, and that the assembly acknowledge the meal as given, not as self-generated — an acknowledgment that leads to gratitude. What this looks like will, of course, vary according to context. To these criteria may be added the more general question of how fully participants engage in the holy transaction of the Supper. Are the words and symbols rich and multivalent, and do the participants allow themselves to be captivated by the images and gestures so that they are open to the transformative power of the Spirit? Strong symbols and active receptivity are both necessary to bind communities of faith together at the eucharist.

Just as a ritual approach to eucharist emphasizes the possibility of transformation of human relationships, so also this approach focuses on the possibility of transformed human-divine relations. According to Calvin and Nevin, union with Christ is the primary purpose of the eucharist. This perspective has the advantage of honoring God's work in and through the event itself, rather than simply seeing it as a secondary human enactment. However, even Calvin and Nevin fall short when it comes to attending to particular celebrations and God's work through them. All the Reformed theologians discussed in chapter one (Calvin, Turretin, Hodge, and Nevin) tended to describe the union of Christ and believer through the eucharist as a definite outcome, provided the proper elements are present. They described union in different ways, and they varied in their estimation of the importance of faith in relation to the objective force of the sacrament. But they agreed on the basic assumption that "the eucharist rightly administered" would accomplish a particular result.[6] Again at this point some

6. Calvin agreed with the Augsburg Confession that the church exists wherever the "gospel is rightly taught and the sacraments are rightly administered" (Augsburg Confession, article vii; cf. Calvin, *Institutes* 4.1.9). This language appears also in the Scots Confession, which outlines three "notes of the church": the true preaching of the Word of God, the right administration of the sacraments, and ecclesiastical discipline (Scots Confession, in *Book of Confessions,* 3.18). This "right administration"

insights of ritual theory may help us to acknowledge the unpredictability of ritual outcomes. Is it enough to claim that the eucharist establishes union between the believer and Christ (by the power of the Spirit) without any attention to what this might look like in particular situations?

As mentioned in chapter three, ritual theorist Catherine Bell turns the claim of God's work in and through the sacrament on its head; she asserts that although ritual participants tend to see their rituals as responding to or transmitting a reality, those rituals actually create the reality of human-divine relationships.[7] The sharp disagreement between ritual theory and theology on this point is, frankly, undecidable. Bell claims that rituals themselves establish relationships; Christian theologians (including the present writer) claim that it is the Holy Spirit who works in and through eucharistic rituals to join participants with Christ. The problem with Bell's argument is that she fails to acknowledge that she herself is making a faith claim in stating that there is no "transcendent" or "divine" realm to be manifested in ritual events. Both Bell's assertion and the Christian perspective presume a type of faith. Bell, with her faith commitment, denies the prior existence of a divine presence. But there is a theological counter-argument from Calvin himself: only if one comes to the eucharist with some "taste of faith" will one be nourished by the Supper of the Lord. Without faith, without receptivity to the work of God in and through the eucharist, the sacrament is ineffective. Bell has already ruled herself out of this sacramental nourishment by her implication that there is no God with whom to be united.[8] So Bell and Christian theologians

---

should be understood in an ample sense, as including ritual adequacy as well as faith of the participants. Even so, to claim that right administration of the sacrament necessarily leads to union with Christ bypasses enormous questions of what concretely constitutes proper administration in each local context.

7. See Catherine Bell, *Ritual: Perspectives and Dimensions* (New York: Oxford University Press, 1997), p. 82.

8. She acknowledges, however, that part of the nature of ritualized behavior is that "ritual agents" perceive themselves as responding to, not creating, transcendent authority. By this analysis, she implicitly recognizes that trust in an authority "beyond the immediate situation" is necessary for ritual effectiveness — a position not unlike Calvin's own assertion that a "taste of faith" is necessary for sacramental nourishment (Bell, *Ritual: Perspectives and Dimensions*, p. 82).

stand in mutually exclusive circles of faith on this point, and neither can convince the other of the accuracy of their perspective.

But if we tread carefully, Bell need not be regarded as utterly hostile to the present project. Even though she herself dismisses the possibility that it is God who works to establish relationship with participants in the eucharist, she clearly respects the power of rituals to establish relationships between humans and a transcendent authority. Though we fundamentally disagree on identity of the ritual agent (the triune God or humanity), we can affirm with Bell that something really happens in the ritual of the eucharist — its power is greater than the sum of the participants' actions. Bell can help Reformed theologians revise their estimation of eucharist as a secondary enactment of prior doctrine, focusing on the power of the eucharistic ritual to establish union of participants with God. Bell would say that the ritual itself unites the participants with "God"; Reformed theologians argue that the Holy Spirit acts in and through the ritual to unite worshipers with Christ. These are two different discourses, but they share a focus on the eucharist as an event in which the faithful are really united with God.

What Does It Mean to Do Theology?

A ritual approach to theology takes its cue from liturgical theologians, who claim that primary theology occurs in the performance of worship, in the adjustment of people to encounter with God. Theology here is not done only in the classroom or the study, but in the midst of the worshiping assembly. Such theology may be called theology *of* rather than theology *about* eucharist. A ritual approach to theology understands itself as secondary, but strives to remain as close as possible to the primary theology, attending to the fine-grained detail of liturgical events, not just texts (as in earlier liturgical theology), abstract form (as in structuralism), meaning (as in some ritual theory), or doctrine (as in too much Reformed theology).

Edward Muir has criticized the sixteenth-century shift in ritual theory, from an emphasis on presenting reality to an emphasis on representation that requires interpretation. In very similar fashion, liturgical theologian Alexander Schmemann has criticized the separation of theology and liturgy that occurred in the sixteenth century. Both

151

scholars were reacting against the Reformation's critical move, the attempt to establish some external point on which to stand to criticize the abuses of the medieval church and its liturgies. Though this move to critique the medieval mass was important at the time, the unfortunate result has been, in its most extreme form, to place all authority in the external reality (theology or interpretation) and demote liturgical action to secondary status. But a ritual approach to eucharistic theology assumes that theology itself occurs in the liturgical event, and it is the responsibility of the reflective theologian to honor that first, observing how the participant theologians are shaping and being shaped by their doings in the assembly.

A ritual approach to eucharistic theology focuses on the liturgical event as a location of God's activity. It therefore honors what goes on in liturgy as theology in the first instance: conversation between people and God, a primary theology that gives rise to secondary reflection. It will be obvious by this time that the claim that God acts in and through the eucharistic celebrations of a community is both a theological assertion and a theological method. If God works through the words and actions of eucharist, then surely we must attend to those words and actions as performed to notice what God may be doing there. We must therefore do theology in a way that takes seriously actual eucharistic practices of a community of faith, rather than always beginning with the secondary reflection and moving into criticism of liturgy as a limited human action that has departed from the ideal form.

This connection between theological claim and theological method can be seen in the two different approaches to eucharist outlined in chapter four. Those who affirmed more strongly God's presence in the sacrament also affirmed more strongly the power of the ritual activity itself. On the other side, those who tended to see God as only tenuously connected to the sacramental activity also tended to claim that the particular eucharistic practices were unimportant. Those who make the theological claim that God works through the eucharist themselves employ the theological method of attending to the details of the eucharistic ritual, while those who claim that God is not particularly bound to the ritual activity tend to discount the eucharistic event itself as having no impact on their theological reflections.

Of course, the balance suggested by Calvin is helpful here: God works in and through the embodied sacramental event, but must not be identified too closely with any particular element or emotion. The anti-idolatry strand within the Reformed tradition, even though it can be overstated, must not be eliminated. Calvin himself, and Turretin and Hodge even more strongly, insisted on maintaining the distinction between God and material elements. In conjunction with this emphasis, they lifted up the role of faith as the necessary receptivity to God's action, so that the sacrament does not operate in some magical way apart from us.[9] Hand in hand with this set of theological assertions goes the theological method that allows secondary, critical theological reflection to inform liturgical practice. Even if we affirm that liturgy is primary theology, we must also acknowledge that liturgy is not God, and therefore there is a place for secondary theology to ask critical questions about what transpires in the liturgical context. The challenge, from the perspective of a ritual approach, is to recall always that the questions asked by secondary theology are themselves shaped by a particular set of primary liturgical practices.

Why Does This Matter?

What is the benefit of this particular approach to eucharistic theology? What good does it do anyone to regard eucharist as a ritual in which God is active? I contend that there are three practical outcomes of this theological perspective.

First, a ritual approach enriches worship itself. By regarding worship as an event that is not entirely within our control, in which God moves to shape and transform us in particular ways, worshipers may attend more carefully to what is going on. They may come to worship with greater anticipation and wonder, hope and gratitude, understanding it as an encounter with the Holy One. It can also relativize

---

9. The constructive balance that Calvin strove to achieve (and that Turretin and Hodge failed to maintain) was to locate the work of God neither in the elements nor in a distant referent, but in usage, in corporate eucharistic action in the community. See Ann Kibbey, *The Interpretation of Material Shapes in Puritanism: A Study of Rhetoric, Prejudice, and Violence* (Cambridge: Cambridge University Press, 1986), pp. 48ff. In this way, Calvin maintained the necessity of material elements and symbolic actions as well as corporate faith, but he did not reduce divine presence to any of these.

the gap between ordained and non-ordained Christians, since all may understand themselves as simultaneously theologians and standing under the radical priority of God.

Secondly, a ritual approach helps to expand our understanding of the Reformed tradition as a theological stream that not only rejects idolatry in worship, but affirms the need for material symbols to communicate God to humanity. It can enrich our sometimes-impoverished anthropology, unify our sometimes-fragmented Christology, emphasize the crucial role of pneumatology, and present a fresh vision of God's divine freedom. First, with regard to anthropology: a ritual approach to eucharist acknowledges that human nature is embodied and therefore that full knowledge of God requires the engagement of all the senses. We do not come to faith only through our ears. We need also to "taste and see that the Lord is good." Second, a ritual approach emphasizes the unity of Christ's natures, following in the footsteps of Nevin, who insisted that in eucharist we are united not only with Christ's divinity but also with his humanity. Third, a ritual approach recovers Calvin's emphasis on the Holy Spirit as the divine power that unites humanity with Christ. Avoiding both localized presence and over-emphasis on faith as human agency, a full pneumatology accounts for the work of God in the actual events of eucharistic celebration, recognizing always that this work is beyond our power to control or predict. And last, a ritual approach to eucharistic theology reinterprets the usual Reformed emphasis on divine freedom as freedom *for* rather than only freedom *from* creation. Divine sovereignty does not mean that God is utterly separated from the world; it means rather that God is not constrained by anything humans can do or imagine.[10] In divine freedom, God has promised to meet us at Supper — not by our actions, and not because of our intellectual comprehension, but because of the free

---

10. This is consistent with Barth's interpretation of divine freedom in passages such as the following: "God's freedom is the freedom proper to and characteristic of Him. It is His freedom not merely to be like the reality different from Himself, but to be as the Creator, Reconciler, and Redeemer acting towards it and in it, and therefore as its sovereign Lord. Again, it is His freedom not merely to be in the differentiation of His being from its being, but to be in Himself the One who can have and hold communion with this reality (as in fact He does) in spite of His utter distinction from it" (*Church Dogmatics* II.1: *The Doctrine of God,* trans. T. F. Torrance and G. W. Bromiley [Edinburgh: T. & T. Clark, 1957], p. 304).

promise of grace. Surely this is one of the clearest instances of Calvin's covenanting God, who comes in the person of Jesus Christ and declares to his disciples, "This cup is the new covenant in my blood."

Finally, a ritual approach to Reformed eucharistic theology presents a new avenue for interreligious conversation: one that begins with doing rather than meaning or believing. We live in a world that is increasingly characterized by religious pluralism, and Christian theologians are called to respond to that situation in a way that is both faithful to our tradition and open to new workings of God's Spirit. Until now, theologians have generally approached the pluralistic situation from a *soteriological* standpoint: Is there salvation outside the church, or apart from Christ?[11] This question has been framed and answered in a variety of ways, but the starting point has been the question of salvation. To this approach has recently been added the voice of liberation theologians, who are concerned primarily with the praxis of liberation in this life.[12] The evolution of liberation theology has prompted some theologians to reframe the issue of interreligious relations as a practical matter, rather than a question about salvation beyond the present life.[13] The question then shifts from a focus on

11. Here, on opposite sides of the argument, may be considered Paul F. Knitter, *No Other Name? A Critical Survey of Christian Attitudes Toward the World Religions* (Maryknoll, N.Y.: Orbis, 1985), esp. chapter 9, and Carl Braaten, *No Other Gospel! Christianity Among the World's Religions* (Minneapolis: Fortress Press, 1992). Jacques Dupuis suggests that this approach characterized most Christian theology before the mid-twentieth century, and lives on in much evangelical Protestant theology today. See Dupuis, *Toward a Christian Theology of Religious Pluralism* (Maryknoll, N.Y.: Orbis, 1997).

12. A classic example of this is Gustavo Gutiérrez, *A Theology of Liberation* (Maryknoll, N.Y.: Orbis, 1973). More recently, Aloysius Pieris has suggested that it is imperative to bring together ethical praxis and interreligious dialogue for a truly Asian liberation theology in *An Asian Theology of Liberation* (Maryknoll, N.Y.: Orbis, 1988), summarized in Dupuis, *Toward a Christian Theology of Religious Pluralism*, pp. 374-37. For an excellent historical overview of Christian approaches to religions, with particular attention to Catholic theologians, see Dupuis, part I.

13. To be sure, "practical" and "soteriological" are not mutually exclusive concerns. Indeed, as liberation theologians have taught us, salvation ought to be a matter of this-worldly well-being at least as much as it is about what happens after death. However, as Dupuis uses these terms, they illuminate an important shift in the primary question of interreligious conversation: from a focus on ultimate status in relation to God to a concern about social and ethical matters in this life.

whether there is salvation through non-Christian religious traditions, to how religious communities can work together in the common struggle for human liberation. This common struggle then calls for "a critical discernment between what in the respective religious traditions constitutes true potential for liberation and what, on the contrary, has been a cause for discrimination and a factor of oppression."[14] Liberation theology has shifted the emphasis from orthodoxy (in the narrow sense) to orthopraxy, and in the process, shifted the questions that Christian theologians ask about other religions.

Like liberation theology, a ritual approach to theology begins with practice. But here the focus is specifically on the ritual practices that form a community in particular ways over time. In the case of eucharistic theology, we have explored how this central ritual practice shapes a worshiping community in attitudes of devotion and communal celebration (even when the eucharistic practices themselves are not acknowledged as important). If this practice shapes persons, then surely it is possible that other religious practices also shape people in particular ways over time. With this move, a ritual approach to interreligious conversation presents a path to dialogue that is simultaneously attentive to our own particularity and open to consideration of the particularity of others.

Of course, a ritual approach to interreligious conversation cannot avoid the tricky question of the relationship between the action of the triune God and human ritual action. In the Reformed Christian tradition, we affirm that the Holy Spirit acts in and through the sacraments because of Christ's institution and the triune God's covenant promise to encounter us in water, bread, and wine. This particular institution and these particular promises are not present in other religious traditions. Does this mean that God does not work through the religious rituals of other peoples of the world? Is there any way to understand non-Christian ritual action in ways that are consistent with the purposes of the triune God? This nexus of issues would have to be addressed by an approach to interreligious dialogue that begins with ritual/liturgical action.

As we have seen, the Reformed tradition is friendly to the idea that we are shaped in crucial ways by liturgical action. This is not an alien

14. Dupuis, *Toward a Christian Theology of Religious Pluralism*, p. 375.

notion introduced by current trends in ritual theory, though the conversation between ritual theorists and Reformed theologians has illumined a theological thread that is often overlooked. If we appreciate the ways in which we ourselves are shaped by the central ritual event of our tradition, perhaps we can appreciate the ways in which others might be ritually formed as well. The question then shifts from "Are you saved?" to "How is your community shaped by ritual action over time in particular attitudes to the world, the neighbor, and the divine?"

In worship, in theological reflection, and in interreligious conversation, then, a ritual approach to eucharistic theology can enrich the Reformed tradition by focusing on doing as primary. This focus on doing, on orthopraxy, can actually lead to an expanded sense of "orthodoxy" as right praise *(doxa)* of God's glory *(doxa)*.[15] As we focus on Christ's presence at table with us, we are "lured and drawn by the ethos of the liturgy to know God's glory."[16] If we continually downplay the significance of ritual, implicitly denying that God can work through the sacramental event to transform individuals and communities, then we withhold parts of ourselves from the influence of the Spirit at the Supper. And indeed, in that case, the Supper will not be transformative. But if we acknowledge the work of God in and through the eucharistic ritual, we are more fully engaged in that event. And as we give more and more of ourselves to that event, we are more and more engrafted into the body of the living Christ. Let us say it again: this is not the result of human agency. It is the result of an increased receptivity, a greater vulnerability to the working of the Holy Spirit. The more we acknowledge that the Spirit really does move through the eucharist, the more responsive we are to that movement.

"Do this in remembrance of me," said Jesus at the Last Supper. "Do this in remembrance of me," says the minister at the eucharist. And so we do, but the doing is not all ours. God does something through our own doing, moving in divine freedom to unite our full humanity to

---

15. As Don Saliers points out, *doxa* has the richly multivalent sense of both human praise and divine glory. "Ortho-doxy" therefore means giving unto God the glory due God's name. See Saliers, *Worship as Theology: Foretaste of Glory Divine* (Nashville: Abingdon Press, 1994), pp. 40f. See also Aidan Kavanagh, *On Liturgical Theology,* The Hale Memorial Lectures of Seabury-Western Theological Seminary, 1981 (Collegeville, Minn.: Liturgical Press, 1984), p. 82.

16. Saliers, *Worship as Theology,* p. 40.

the fullness of Christ. Sometimes this happens quickly, but more often it happens over time, as the Holy Spirit gradually draws us into closer union with the One who gave us birth, who feeds us with his own body, and who beckons to us from the brightness of divine glory at the end of time.

Questionnaire on Communion

Questions About Your Experience of Communion

1. How many times do you take communion in an average year?

   1-2   3-4   5-6   7-8   9-10   11-12   13+

2. If you know that First Presbyterian is going to be celebrating communion on a Sunday, are you more or less likely to attend worship?
   - ☐ More likely
   - ☐ Less likely
   - ☐ Doesn't matter

3. Do you think First Presbyterian celebrates communion . . . ? (Check one.)
   - ☐ Too often
   - ☐ Not often enough
   - ☐ About the right amount

4. What word best describes the mood of the congregation at First Presbyterian during communion?
   - ☐ Quiet and somber
   - ☐ Joyful
   - ☐ Peaceful
   - ☐ Other: _____

5. What do you think *ought to be* the mood of the congregation during communion?

   ☐ Quiet and somber

   ☐ Joyful

   ☐ Peaceful

   ☐ Other: _____

6. What is the meaning of the Lord's Supper for you?
   (Rank up to 3, with 1 as most meaningful.)

   ☐ Has little meaning

   ☐ Reminds us of the Last Supper of Jesus and his death

   ☐ Unites us with the body of Christ

   ☐ Calls us into fellowship with each other

   ☐ Cleanses us of our sins

   ☐ Looks forward to the joyful banquet of the Lord at the end of time

   ☐ Other: _____

7. What is the most important part of communion for you? (Check one.)

   ☐ The minister's prayer

   ☐ The Words of Institution ("this is my body . . .")

   ☐ Eating and drinking

   ☐ Seeing the minister break the bread and pour the wine

   ☐ Serving

   ☐ Private individual prayer

   ☐ Other: _____

8. At First Presbyterian, we usually receive the bread and juice while sitting in the pews. Have you ever attended a communion service in which the elements were given in a different way?

   Yes   No   *(If you answered "no," please skip to question 9.)*

8a. What other ways have you participated in communion? (Check as many as apply.)

☐ Intinction (going forward and dipping bread into cup)

☐ Going forward and receiving elements individually from minister or priest

☐ Serving self

☐ Passing bread and cup around a circle

☐ Other: _____

8b. Of the modes of communion in which you have participated, which was most meaningful to you? Why?

_____

_____

_____

9. What do you usually do while the communion elements are being distributed? (Rank up to 3, with 1 being the most frequent activity.)

☐ Pray

☐ Listen to the music

☐ Meditate on the bread and juice as I hold and consume them

☐ Look at the people around me

☐ Watch the servers

☐ Get impatient

☐ Other: _____

10. Which scripture is most important in helping you think about communion? (Circle one.)

Matthew 26:26-29:
"While they were eating, Jesus took a loaf of bread, and after blessing it he broke it, gave it to the disciples, and said, 'Take, eat; this is my body.' Then he took a cup, and after giving thanks he gave it to them, saying, 'Drink from it, all of you; for this is my blood of the covenant, which is poured out for many for the forgiveness of sins. I

tell you, I will never again drink of this fruit of the vine until that day when I drink it new with you in my Father's kingdom.'"

Luke 24:28-31:
[On the road to Emmaus] "As they came near the village to which they were going, he walked ahead as if he were going on. But they urged him strongly, saying, 'Stay with us, because it is almost evening and the day is now nearly over.' So he went in to stay with them. When he was at table with them, he took bread, blessed and broke it, and gave it to them. Then their eyes were opened, and they recognized him; and he vanished from their sight."

John 6:35:
"Jesus said to them, 'I am the bread of life. Whoever comes to me will never be hungry, and whoever believes in me will never be thirsty.'"

1 Corinthians 11:23-26:
"For I received from the Lord what I also handed on to you, that the Lord Jesus on the night when he was betrayed took a loaf of bread, and when he had given thanks, he broke it and said, 'This is my body that is for you. Do this in remembrance of me.' In the same way he took the cup also, after supper, saying, 'This cup is the new covenant in my blood. Do this, as often as you drink it, in remembrance of me.' For as often as you eat this bread and drink this cup, you proclaim the Lord's death until he comes."

☐ Other: _____

11. In which of the following settings at First Presbyterian have you participated in communion? (Check all that apply.)

☐ Chapel (old sanctuary)

☐ Fellowship Hall

☐ New Sanctuary

☐ Retreat

☐ Other: _____

11a. Of the above locations, which has been your favorite place for celebrating communion? Why?

_____

_____

_____

12. What kind of music do you think is most appropriate during communion? (Check one)
    ☐ No music at all
    ☐ Organ or piano alone
    ☐ Vocal solo
    ☐ Choir
    ☐ Congregational singing
    ☐ Other: _____

    12a. If music is part of the communion service, do you think that music should be:
        ☐ Joyous
        ☐ Quiet and reflective
        ☐ Somber
        ☐ Varied
        ☐ Other: _____

13. According to your memory, when communion is celebrated, is it mentioned in the sermon?

    Never   occasionally   usually   always   can't remember

14. According to your memory, when communion is celebrated, are the hymns related to that occasion?

    Never   occasionally   usually   always   can't remember

15. According to your memory, when communion is celebrated, are the prayers related to that occasion?

    Never   occasionally   usually   always   can't remember

16. Are there other occasions in the church's life when you think of communion? If so, when?

_____

_____

_____

17. Are there any other comments you would like to make about your experience of or thoughts on communion at First Presbyterian?

_____

_____

_____

Demographic Information

18. Gender

    M   F

19. Age

    17-25   26-35   36-45   46-55   56-65   66-75   76+

20. How many years have you been a member of this church?

    1-4   5-10   11-15   16-20   21-25   26+

21. Check the statement that best represents your level of involvement at First Presbyterian:
    ☐ I occasionally come to worship.
    ☐ I regularly come to worship.
    ☐ I regularly come to worship and participate in one other activity (e.g., Sunday school, choir, Bible study).
    ☐ I regularly come to worship and participate in at least two other activities.

22. In what religious tradition were you raised? If you were raised in more than one, with which did you have the greatest identification?

    None   Roman Catholic   Episcopalian   Methodist

    Baptist   Presbyterian   Lutheran   Pentecostal   Jewish

    Other: _____

Thank you for your help!

Results of Questionnaire

Number of surveys mailed:	*163*
Number of surveys returned:	*115*
Response rate:	*71%*

1. How many times do you take communion in an average year?

1 to 2	*7%*
3 to 4	*35%*
5 to 6	*22%*
7 to 8	*12%*
9 to 10	*16%*
11 to 12	*4%*
13 or more	*1%*
As often as given	*4%*

2. If you know that First Presbyterian is going to be celebrating communion on a Sunday, are you more or less likely to attend worship?

More likely	*46%*
Less likely	*—*
Doesn't matter	*54%*

3. Do you think First Presbyterian celebrates communion . . . ?
(Check one.)

Too often   *1%*

Not often enough   *15%*

About the right amount *84%*

4. What word best describes the mood of the congregation at First
Presbyterian during communion?

Quiet and somber   *53%*

Joyful   *1%*

Peaceful   *42%*

Other   *2%*

Don't know   *3%*

5. What do you think *ought to be* the mood of the congregation
during communion?

Quiet and somber   *34%*

Joyful   *10%*

Peaceful   *52%*

Other   *4%*

Don't know   —

6. What is the meaning of the Lord's Supper for you?
(Rank up to 3, with 1 as most meaningful.)

	n=114 first most meaningful	n=95 second most	n=81 third most
Has little meaning	—	—	—
Reminds us of the Last Supper of Jesus and his death	*41%*	*28%*	*17%*
Unites us with the body of Christ	*43%*	*27%*	*14%*

167

Calls us into fellowship with each other

| | 6% | 15% | 35% |

Cleanses us of our sins

| | 8% | 18% | 20% |

Looks forward to the joyful banquet of the Lord at the end of time

| | 1% | 8% | 11% |

Other

| | 1% | 3% | 4% |

7. What is the most important part of communion for you? (Check one.)

The minister's prayer	5%
The Words of Institution ("this is my body . . .")	50%
Eating and drinking	5%
Seeing the minister break the bread and pour the wine	7%
Serving	1%
Private individual prayer	30%
Other	3%

8. At First Presbyterian, we usually receive the bread and juice while sitting in the pews. Have you ever attended a communion service in which the elements were given in a different way?

| Yes | 89% |
| No (skip to question 9) | 11% |

8a. What other ways have you participated in communion?
(Check as many as apply.)

n (number of respondents eligible to answer this question) = 213
(percentages add to more than 100 because respondents could make
more than one response)

Intinction (going forward and dipping bread into cup)   29%

Going forward and receiving elements individually
from minister or priest   51%

Serving self   9%

Passing bread and cup around a circle   11%

Other   1%

8b. Of the modes of communion in which you have
participated, which was most meaningful to you? Why?

n=74

Intinction (going forward and dipping bread into cup)   5%

Going forward and receiving elements individually
from minister or priest   34%

Serving self   4%

Passing bread and cup around a circle   7%

Other   8%

Pews   36%

All   5%

9. What do you usually do while the communion elements are being distributed? (Rank up to 3, with 1 being the most frequent activity.)

	n=113 first most frequent	n=93 second most frequent	n=63 third most frequent
Pray	50%	28%	14%
Listen to the music	13%	30%	48%
Meditate on the bread and juice as I hold and consume them	30%	37%	21%
Look at the people around me	4%	1%	3%
Watch the servers	2%	2%	11%
Get impatient	—	—	—
Other	2%	2%	3%

10. Which scripture is most important in helping you think about communion? (check one)

Matthew 26:26-29	60%
Luke 24:28-31	—
John 6:35	7%
1 Corinthians 11:23-26	33%
Other	—

11. In which of the following settings at First Presbyterian have you participated in communion? (Check all that apply.)

> **n=325** (percentages add to more than 100 because respondents could make more than one response)

Chapel (old sanctuary)	98%
Fellowship Hall	77%
New sanctuary	85%
Retreat	26%
Other	2%

11a. Of the above locations, which has been your favorite place(s) for celebrating communion? Why?

	n=159
Chapel (old sanctuary)	44%
Fellowship Hall	1%
New sanctuary	27%
Retreat	15%
Other	—
All	13%

12. What kind of music do you think is most appropriate during communion? (Check one.)

No music at all	4%
Organ or piano alone	86%
Vocal solo	—
Choir	3%
Congregational singing	4%
Other	3%

12a. If music is part of the communion service,
do you think that music should be:

Joyous	4%
Quiet and reflective	86%
Somber	2%
Varied	9%
Other	—

13. According to your memory, when communion is celebrated, is it mentioned in the sermon?

Never	—
Occasionally	24%
Usually	46%
Always	16%
Can't remember	14%

14. According to your memory, when communion is celebrated, are the hymns related to that occasion?

Never	—
Occasionally	15%
Usually	61%
Always	15%
Can't remember	9%

15. According to your memory, when communion is celebrated, are the prayers related to that occasion?

Never	—
Occasionally	11%
Usually	55%
Always	26%
Can't remember	8%

16. Are there other occasions in the church's life when you think of communion? If so, when?

    n=41 (percentages add to more than 100 because respondents could make more than one response)

Baptisms	10%
Retreats	2%
Christmas/Christmas Eve	39%
Easter/Easter Week/Lent/Maundy Thursday	46%
Death/funeral	22%
Wedding	27%
New members joining/confirmation	10%
Other	37%

17. Are there any other comments you would like to make about your experience of or thoughts on communion at First Presbyterian?

    (not tabulated)

Demographic Information

18. Gender

Male	30%
Female	70%

19. Age

17 to 25 years	1%
26 to 35 years	8%
36 to 45 years	14%
46 to 55 years	14%
56 to 65 years	10%
66 to 75 years	27%
76 years or more	27%

20. How many years have you been a member of First Presbyterian?

1 to 4 years	20%
5 to 10 years	29%
11 to 15 years	11%
16 to 20 years	12%
21 to 25 years	10%
26 years or more	18%

21. Check the statement that best represents your level of involvement at First Presbyterian:

I occasionally come to worship.	22%
I regularly come to worship.	28%
I regularly come to worship and participate in one other activity (e.g., Sunday school, choir, Bible study).	26%
I regularly come to worship and participate in at least two other activities.	24%

22. In what religious tradition were you raised?
    If you were raised in more than one, with which
    did you have the greatest identification?

Presbyterian	38%
Methodist	23%
Baptist	18%
Episcopalian	8%
Lutheran	6%
Other	6%

Bibliography

Anderson, E. Byron, and Bruce T. Morrill, eds. *Liturgy and the Moral Self: Humanity at Full Stretch Before God.* Collegeville, Minn.: Liturgical Press, 1998.

Anderson, Herbert, and Edward Foley. *Mighty Stories, Dangerous Rituals: Weaving Together the Human and the Divine.* San Francisco: Jossey-Bass Publishers, 1998.

Baillie, Donald. *The Theology of the Sacraments and Other Papers.* New York: Charles Scribner's Sons, 1957.

Bauman, Richard. *Verbal Art as Performance.* Prospect Heights, Ill.: Waveland Press, Inc., 1977.

Bell, Catherine. *Ritual Theory, Ritual Practice.* New York: Oxford University Press, 1992.

———. *Ritual: Perspectives and Dimensions.* New York: Oxford University Press, 1997.

Berger, Teresa. "Prayers and Practices of Women: Lex Orandi Reconfigured." In *Women, Ritual, and Liturgy,* edited by Susan K. Roll, Annette Esser, et al., pp. 63-77. Yearbook of the European Society of Women in Theological Research. Louvain: Peeters, 2001.

Book of Church Order of the Presbyterian Church in the United States. Richmond: Presbyterian Committee of Publication, [1921?].

Book of Church Order of the Presbyterian Church in the United States. Revised edition. Richmond: Presbyterian Committee of Publication, 1945.

Book of Common Worship. Presbyterian Church in the United States of America. 1946.

The Book of Common Worship: Provisional Services and Lectionary for the Christian Year. Joint Committee on Worship, Cumberland Presbyterian Church, Presbyterian Church in the United States and United Presbyterian Church in the United States of America. Philadelphia: Westminster Press, 1966.

Book of Common Worship. Presbyterian Church (USA). Louisville: Westminster/ John Knox Press, 1993.

Book of Confessions: Study Edition. Louisville: Geneva Press, 1996.

Book of Order (1983-85). Atlanta and New York: Presbyterian Church (USA), 1983.

Book of Order (2005-2007). Louisville: Presbyterian Church (USA), 2005.

Briggs, Charles. *Competence in Performance: The Creativity of Tradition in Mexicano Verbal Art.* Philadelphia: University of Pennsylvania Press, 1988.

―――. "'Since I Am a Woman, I Will Chastise My Relatives': Gender, Reported Speech, and the (Re)production of Social Relations." *American Ethnologist* 19 (1992): 337-61.

Calvin, John. *Institutes of the Christian Religion.* Edited by John T. McNeill. Library of Christian Classics, XX-XXI. Philadelphia: Westminster Press, 1960.

―――. *Commentaries.* Edited by Joseph Haroutunian and Louise Pettibone Smith. Library of Christian Classics, XXIII. Philadelphia: Westminster Press, 1958.

―――. "Short Treatise on the Holy Supper." In *Theological Treatises,* edited by J. K. S. Reid, pp. 140-66. Library of Christian Classics, XXII. Philadelphia: Westminster Press, 1954.

―――. *The Gospel According to St. John 1–10.* Translated by T. H. L. Parker. Edited by David W. Torrance and Thomas F. Torrance. Calvin's Commentaries. Edinburgh: Oliver & Boyd, 1959.

―――. *The Epistles of Paul the Apostle to the Galatians, Ephesians, Philippians, and Colossians.* Translated by T. H. L. Parker. Edited by David W. Torrance and Thomas F. Torrance. Calvin's Commentaries. Edinburgh: Oliver & Boyd, 1965.

―――. "The Form of Church Prayers, Strassburg, 1545, and Geneva, 1542." In *Liturgies of the Western Church,* selected and introduced by Bard Thompson, pp. 185-210. Cleveland: William Collins and World Publishing Co., 1961.

Collins, Mary. *Worship: Renewal to Practice.* Washington, D.C.: Pastoral Press, 1987.

de Clerck, Paul. "'Lex orandi, lex credendi': Sens original et avatars historiques d'un adage équivoque." *Questions Liturgiques* 59 (1978): 193-212. Translated into English as "'Lex orandi, lex credendi': The Original Sense and Historical Avatars of an Equivocal Adage." *Studia Liturgica* 24 (1994): 178-200.

De Coppet, Daniel, ed. *Understanding Rituals.* London: Routledge, 1992.

Dix, Dom Gregory. *The Shape of the Liturgy.* Westminster: Dacre, 1945.

Driver, Tom. *Liberating Rites: Understanding the Transformative Power of Ritual.* Boulder: Westview Press, 1998.

Dupuis, Jacques. *Toward a Christian Theology of Religious Pluralism.* Maryknoll, N.Y.: Orbis, 1997.

Elwood, Christopher. *The Body Broken: The Calvinist Doctrine of the Eucharist and the Symbolization of Power in Sixteenth-Century France.* New York: Oxford University Press, 1999.

Fagerberg, David. *What Is Liturgical Theology? A Study in Methodology.* Collegeville, Minn.: Liturgical Press, 1992.

Falconer, Alan D. "Word, Sacrament, and Communion: New Emphases in Reformed Worship in the Twentieth Century." In *Christian Worship in Reformed Churches Past and Present,* edited by Lukas Vischer, pp. 142-58. Grand Rapids: Eerdmans, 2003.

Geertz, Clifford. *The Interpretation of Cultures.* New York: Basic Books, 1973.

George, Timothy. *Theology of the Reformers.* Nashville: Broadman Press, 1988.

Gerrish, Brian. *Grace and Gratitude: The Eucharistic Theology of John Calvin.* Minneapolis: Fortress Press, 1993.

Grimes, Ronald L. *Beginnings in Ritual Studies.* Washington, D.C.: University Press of America, 1982.

———. *Ritual Criticism: Case Studies in Its Practice, Essays on Its Theory.* Columbia: University of South Carolina Press, 1991.

———. "Liturgical Renewal and Ritual Criticism." In *The Awakening Church,* edited by Lawrence J. Madden, pp. 11-25. Collegeville, Minn.: Liturgical Press, 1992.

Hageman, Howard G. *Pulpit and Table: Some Chapters in the History of Worship in the Reformed Churches.* Richmond: John Knox Press, 1962.

Hamstra, Sam, Jr., and Arie J. Griffioen, eds. *Reformed Confessionalism in Nineteenth Century America.* Lanham, Md.: Scarecrow Press, 1995.

Handelman, Don. *Models and Mirrors: Toward an Anthropology of Public Events.* Cambridge: Cambridge University Press, 1990.

Heron, Alasdair I. C. *Table and Tradition: Toward an Ecumenical Understanding of the Eucharist.* Philadelphia: Westminster Press, 1983.

Hick, John. *A Christian Theology of Religions: The Rainbow of Faiths.* Louisville: Westminster/John Knox Press, 1995.

Hick, John, and Paul F. Knitter, eds. *The Myth of Christian Uniqueness: Toward a Pluralistic Theology of Religions.* Maryknoll, N.Y.: Orbis Books, 1989.

Hodge, Charles. Review of *The Mystical Presence. Princeton Review* 20 (April 1848): 227-78.

Holifield, E. Brooks. *The Covenant Sealed: The Development of Puritan Sacramental Theology in Old and New England, 1570-1720.* New York and London: Yale University Press, 1974.

———. "Mercersburg, Princeton, and the South: The Sacramental Controversy in the Nineteenth Century." *Journal of Presbyterian History* 54 (Summer 1976): 238-57.

Irwin, Kevin. *Context and Text: Method in Liturgical Theology.* Collegeville, Minn.: Liturgical Press, 1994.

Jasper, R. C. D., and G. J. Cuming. *Prayers of the Eucharist: Early and Reformed.* 3rd rev. ed. Collegeville, Minn.: Liturgical Press, 1990.

Jennings, Theodore W., Jr. "Ritual Studies and Liturgical Theology: An Invitation to Dialogue." *Journal of Ritual Studies* 1, no. 1 (1987): 43-45.

Jones, Cheslyn, Geoffrey Wainwright, et al., eds. *The Study of Liturgy.* Rev. ed. London: SPCK, 1992.

Kavanagh, Aidan. *On Liturgical Theology.* Collegeville, Minn.: Liturgical Press, 1984.

———. "Response [to Geoffrey Wainwright]: Primary Theology and Liturgical Act." *Worship* 57 (July 1983): 309-24.

Kay, James. "The Lex Orandi in Recent Protestant Theology." In *Ecumenical Theology in Worship, Doctrine, and Life: Essays Presented to Geoffrey Wainwright on His Sixtieth Birthday,* edited by David S. Cunningham, Ralph del Colle, and Lucas Lamadrid, pp. 11-23. New York: Oxford University Press, 1999.

Kertzer, David I. *Ritual, Politics, and Power.* New Haven: Yale University Press, 1988.

Kibbey, Ann. *The Interpretation of Material Shapes in Puritanism: A Study of Rhetoric, Prejudice, and Violence.* Cambridge: Cambridge University Press, 1986.

Knitter, Paul F. *No Other Name? A Critical Survey of Christian Attitudes Toward the World Religions.* Maryknoll, N.Y.: Orbis Books, 1992.

Lathrop, Gordon. *Holy Things: A Liturgical Theology.* Minneapolis: Fortress Press, 1993.

———. *Holy People: A Liturgical Ecclesiology.* Minneapolis: Fortress Press, 1999.

Lindbeck, George. *The Nature of Doctrine: Religion and Theology in a Postliberal Age.* Philadelphia: Westminster Press, 1984.

Madden, Lawrence J., ed. *The Awakening Church: 25 Years of Liturgical Renewal.* Collegeville, Minn.: Liturgical Press, 1992.

Marshall, Paul V. "Reconsidering 'Liturgical Theology': Is There a *Lex Orandi* for All Christians?" *Studia Liturgica* 25 (1995): 129-51.

Maxwell, Jack Martin. *Worship and Reformed Theology: The Liturgical Lessons of Mercersburg.* Pittsburgh: The Pickwick Press, 1976.

McDonnell, Kilian. *John Calvin, the Church, and the Eucharist.* Princeton: Princeton University Press, 1967.

McKee, Elsie Anne. "Reformed Worship in the Sixteenth Century." In *Christian Worship in Reformed Churches Past and Present,* edited by Lukas Vischer, pp. 3-31. Grand Rapids: Eerdmans, 2003.

Muir, Edward. *Ritual in Early Modern Europe*. Cambridge: Cambridge University Press, 1997.

Murken, Todd B. *Take and Eat, and Take the Consequences: How Receiving the Lord's Supper Is an Action That Makes a Difference*. New York: Peter Lang, 2002.

Nevin, John Williamson. *The Mystical Presence: A Vindication of the Reformed or Calvinistic Doctrine of the Holy Eucharist*. Originally published, Philadelphia: J. B. Lippincott & Co., 1846; reprinted, Eugene, Oregon: Wipf & Stock, 2000.

Nichols, James Hastings. *Corporate Worship in the Reformed Tradition*. Philadelphia: Westminster Press, 1968.

Old, Hughes Oliphant. *Worship That Is Reformed According to Scripture*. Guides to the Reformed Tradition, John H. Leith and John W. Kuykendall, series editors. Atlanta: John Knox Press, 1984.

Phillips, Timothy. "The Dissolution of Francis Turretin's Vision of *Theologia*: Geneva at the End of the Seventeenth Century." In *The Identity of Geneva: The Christian Commonwealth 1564-1864*, edited by John B. Roney and Martin I. Klauber, pp. 77-92. Westport, Conn.: Greenwood Press, 1998.

Raheja, Gloria Goodwin, and Ann Grodzins Gold. *Listen to the Heron's Words: Reimagining Gender and Kinship in North India*. Berkeley: University of California Press, 1994.

Rappaport, Roy A. "The Obvious Aspects of Ritual." In *Ecology, Meaning, and Religion*. Richmond, Calif.: North Atlantic Books, 1979.

Saliers, Don E. *Worship as Theology: Foretaste of Glory Divine*. Nashville: Abingdon Press, 1994.

Sasse, Hermann. *This Is My Body: Luther's Contention for the Real Presence in the Sacrament of the Altar*. Minneapolis: Augsburg Publishing House, 1959.

Schmemann, Alexander. "Liturgy and Theology." *Greek Orthodox Theological Review* 17, no. 1 (1972): 86-100.

———. *Introduction to Liturgical Theology*. Translated by Ashleigh Moorhouse. London: The Faith Press, 1966.

Small, Joseph D. "A Church of the Word and Sacrament." In *Christian Worship in Reformed Churches Past and Present*, edited by Lukas Vischer, pp. 311-23. Grand Rapids: Eerdmans, 2003.

Staal, Frits. "The Meaninglessness of Ritual." *Numen* 26, no. 1 (1975): 2-22.

Taft, Robert. "The Structural Analysis of Liturgical Units: An Essay in Methodology." *Worship* 52, no. 4 (July 1978): 314-29.

———. "Liturgy as Theology." *Worship* 56, no. 2 (March 1982): 113-17.

Tambiah, Stanley. *A Performative Approach to Ritual*. Radcliffe-Brown Lecture 1979. London: For the British Academy by Oxford University Press, 1981.

Tillich, Paul. *Christianity and the Encounter of World Religions*. Minneapolis: Fortress Press, 1994. Originally published, New York: Columbia University Press, 1963.

Turner, Victor. *The Ritual Process: Structure and Anti-Structure.* New York: Aldine de Gruyter, 1995. Originally published, Chicago: Aldine Publishing Company, 1969.

————. *The Anthropology of Performance.* New York: Performing Arts Journal Publications, 1988.

Turretin, Francis. *Institutes of Elenctic Theology,* vol. 3. Translated by George Musgrave Giger. Edited by James T. Dennison, Jr. Phillipsburg, N.J.: Presbyterian and Reformed Publishing Company, 1997.

von Allmen, Jean-Jacques. *Worship: Its Theology and Practice.* New York: Oxford University Press, 1965.

Wainwright, Geoffrey. *Doxology: The Praise of God in Worship, Doctrine, and Life: A Systematic Theology.* New York: Oxford University Press, 1980.

Wallace, Peter J. "History and Sacrament: John Williamson Nevin and Charles Hodge on the Lord's Supper." *Mid-America Journal of Theology* 11 (2000): 171-201.

Wallace, Ronald S. *Calvin's Doctrine of the Word and Sacrament.* Edinburgh: Oliver & Boyd, 1953.

White, James F. *Sacraments as God's Self-Giving: Sacramental Practice and Faith.* Nashville: Abingdon Press, 1983.

————. *Protestant Worship: Traditions in Transition.* Louisville: Westminster/ John Knox Press, 1989.

Wilfong, Marsha M. "Reformed Worship in the United States of America." In *Christian Worship in Reformed Churches Past and Present,* edited by Lukas Vischer, pp. 107-41. Grand Rapids: Eerdmans, 2003.

The Worshipbook. Joint Committee on Worship, Cumberland Presbyterian Church, Presbyterian Church in the United States and United Presbyterian Church in the United States of America. Philadelphia: Westminster Press, 1970.

Index

Index

Holy Spirit, 30, 41-42; and emergence, 101; and John Calvin's understanding, 16, 24-25, 41-42; and relationship of people 25, 96-97; and the Lord's Supper, 157

India: and women's songs, 99-100; Holi, 103-4
Interreligious conversation, 155-58
Interviews, results of, 110, 112, 128-29, 130-32, 134-35
Invitation to the Lord's Supper, 112-15
Irwin, Kevin, 67-68, 77-78

Jennings, Theodore, 78

Kavanagh, Aidan, 63, 71, 81, 84
Kertzer, David, 101

Lathrop, Gordon, 74-76, 79-80, 110
Lex agendi, 85, 87-106. *See also Lex orandi, lex credendi*
Lex orandi, lex credendi, 63-69, 121; and change of understanding, 64, and critique of formulation, 65-67; and local considerations, 108-9; as established by practice 68-69, fourfold approach 109-11. *See also Lex agendi*
Lindbeck, George, 11n.4
Liturgical theology, 61-62, 69-70; and critique, 77-83
Liturgy: and active participation, 138; and *leitourgia,* 74; and understanding, 31-32; as primary theology, 12, 70-73; as secondary theology, 12
Local practices and the Lord's Supper, 108
Lord's Supper; and baptism, 112-15; and faith, 47-48, 54-55, 59, 121; and signs, 48; and social order, 105-6; converting power of, 31-32;

corporate action in, 137-40; distribution of, 127-33; fourfold action of, 92; individual devotion approach to, 130-33, 134-37; invitation to, 112-15; meditative approach to, 130-33; remembrance as theme of, 124-26; spiritual presence in, 38-39; union with Christ as theme of, 55-58
Luther, Martin, 16-19
Lutheran view of the elements, 24

Marburg Colloquy, 16-19
Marks of the church, 22n.20
Marshall, Paul, 65
McDonnell, Kilian, 25n.25, 33, 39, 41-42
McKee, Elsie Anne, 35
Monophysite argument, 19n.12
Muir, Edward, 15, 89-90, 98, 137
Music and the Lord's Supper, 134
Mystical union, 55-58

Nestorian argument, 19n.12
Nevin, John Williamson, 49-58, 61, 144, 154
Nominalism, 40n.74, 96-97

Oecolampadius, 17

Performance theory, 98
Phenomenological observation, 109
Primary theology, 70-73, 84
Prosper of Aquitaine, 63, 66
Protestant Scholasticism, 45-49

Raheja, Gloria, 99
Rappaport, Roy, 90-91, 93
Reflection during distribution, 130-33
Reformation, 15-16, 137
Ricoeur, Paul, 141
Ritual studies, 78-79

183

INDEX